160 WAYS TO HELP THE WORLD

Community Service Projects for Young People

LINDA LEEB DUPER

Facts On File, Inc.
AN INFOBASE HOLDINGS COMPANY

160 Ways to Help the World: Community Service Projects for Young People

Copyright © 1996 by Linda Leeb Duper

Facts On File, Inc.
11 Penn Plaza
New York NY 10001

Library of Congress Cataloging-in-Publication Data

Duper, Linda Leeb.
    160 ways to help the world : community service projects for young people /
Linda Leeb Duper.
        p. cm.
    Includes bibliographical references and index.
    ISBN 0-8160-3324-2 (hb : alk. paper), ISBN 0-8160-3503-2 (pb)
    1. Children as volunteers—Juvenile literature.   2. Social action—Juvenile literature.
3. Voluntarism—Juvenile literature.
    I. Title.
HQ784.V64D86   1996
361.3'7—dc20   95-34223

Text design by Catherine Rincon Hyman
Jacket design by Leah Lococo

This book is printed on acid-free paper.

Printed in the United States of America

MP FOF 10 9 8 7 6 5 4 3 2 1

Everyone can be great,
because everyone can serve.

—Rev. Martin Luther King, Jr.

Contents

Acknowledgments

I would like to thank the following organizations and individuals for their help: Alameda County Social Services; Alta Bates Medical Center; Berkeley-Oakland Support Services (BOSS); Oakland Children's Hospital; Oakland Public Libraries; Project Yes; Quest International; A Safe Place for Women; University of California, Berkeley; Bahá'ís everywhere, especially in Oakland; Beth-Ann Berliner; Kathleen Stratman York; my husband Carson; my sister Patricia; my friend Elisa; my former students; and all the millions of people in the world who serve the oneness of humanity.

There are others, and they know who they are, but I have to stop somewhere.

1

What Is Community Service and Why Should You Do It?

> No one can be perfectly free till all are free; no one can be perfectly moral till all are moral; no one can be perfectly happy till all are happy.
>
> —Herbert Spencer, *Social Statics*

Your Community: You Can't Leave It, So You Better Love It

The dictionary defines a community as "any group living in the same area or having interests, work, etc. in common." When we speak of community, we usually mean the first part of the definition—the physical area (block, neighborhood, town, and so forth) where we live and work. But the second part of the definition is equally important, and in some ways has larger and more interesting implications.

It's easy to see how we're connected to and affected by the people who live in our immediate surroundings. If the block is shabby and dirty, everyone on the block has to look at it and wade through the debris. If the neighborhood isn't safe, everyone's at risk. If the city is badly governed, everyone in town suffers.

When we extend our idea of our community to include not just the people who live around us but also those with whom we have interests in common, we ally ourselves with a whole new world of people, places, and concerns we may not have thought of as having any relationship to us. Our world expands, and we start to realize that we're all connected in some way. For example, if you're a student and the nation's schools are in trouble, you have something in common with every student in the country. The students of America can be called a community, of which you are a part. If you're a musician (or engineer or farmer or parent), you're part of a group that transcends geographical boundaries and links you to other musicians (engineers, farmers, parents) throughout the world. Your goals, interests, setbacks, and successes are shared and have an effect that may be felt throughout your community. If you have a hit song, the music market changes, affecting other musicians. New developments in engineering in Canada change the way bridges are built in Saudi Arabia.

Let's take this idea even further. Everyone in the world needs clean air to breathe, clean water to drink, and protection from the sun's ultraviolet rays. We all share these interests, regardless of race, nationality, or any other man-made category. The forces of nature don't care about national boundaries or political affiliations. If the air and water are polluted or the ozone layer is damaged, everyone suffers—American or Algerian, Democrat or Republican. When we look at it this way, we see that we're all part of a world community. We're all affected by the same phenomena.

To look at it more positively, we all profit from the same advantages. A clean, safe neighborhood makes life easier and more pleasant for everyone on the block. A well-governed town provides useful services to all its citizens. A cleaner environment makes a healthier world for all humanity.

When you look at it this way, your community extends from your bedroom door to the farthest reaches of the globe. So even something you do locally, just in your neighborhood or town, can help the world. When you help make the air a little cleaner or help save a few oxygen-producing trees by recycling in your school or neighborhood, you're actually helping the whole world. Your community just got a whole lot bigger—and better. And you've made a difference to your community all over the planet.

Service: A Little Help for Our Friends

This brings us to the idea of *service*. Since others are part of your community, when you do something for them, you also do something for yourself. So there's an element of self-interest in service, once you realize that your interests are tied to those of others. When you help your community, you help yourself.

Community service makes you realize how important *everyone* is. You begin to see clearly that your own well-being is inextricably linked to that of others, and that what you do affects others, and vice versa. Service highlights your own importance in your community. Sometimes it may not seem as though you're all that important or that your voice is heard, but when you perform community service, no matter how small it may seem, it helps you realize how important you are, what a vital part of our communities we all are. There's nothing like having an effect to make you realize the importance of your actions. The more you help make your world a better place, the more important you become in that world.

But Does It Really Work?

Yes, it really works. (What did you expect me to say?) Community service, also called volunteer work, can accomplish amazing things. The power of people working together in a spirit of concern for others and enlightened self-interest is one of our most valuable resources—and it has been used throughout history to do exceptionally important work.

The United States has a long and fruitful history of volunteer community service. Most of the great victories for freedom and human rights and other excellent ideals came about because thousands of people just like you freely gave their time and effort to these causes. These great movements were the result of lots of people who all did their bit—however great or small—to make life better for others and, by extension, for themselves.

In fact, you could say this country was created through the efforts of volunteers. The Minutemen, who fought the British during the Revolutionary War, were all volunteers—farmers, merchants, and craftspeople who gave their time, energy, and sometimes their lives to make the nation independent. They knew it was up to them to make the kind of country they wanted.

The freeing of the slaves came about in part because of the abolitionist movement, which was composed of groups of everyday people whose united efforts influenced every level of society, from field workers to the president. Like Herbert Spencer, a social reformer quoted at the beginning of this chapter, they knew that a society capable of enslaving any of its members could not be truly free for anyone, and they exerted pressure on the government and the slaveholders until they achieved their goal of freedom for all.

Civil rights, equal rights for women, child-protection laws, humane treatment of animals, the preservation of the environment—all of these noble causes grew and became part of our culture through the efforts of volunteers performing service of some kind. Few will dispute that they have made our world a better place, and their beneficial effect on all of us is undeniable. It can be said that we are profiting from the efforts of volunteers long dead and gone. If we expend this same kind of effort, someone in the future may have a better life because of it. So if you think community service isn't all that important, or that it doesn't have a lasting effect, think again.

Great Expectations

All of this doesn't mean you now have to rush out and save the world with some grand, heroic deed. The idea is that we all do whatever we can *reasonably* do, and it all adds up to something wonderful and useful. It's true that the *Titanic* has been littering the ocean floor for some time now, but we don't expect you to raise it single-handedly. It's not reasonable to expect you to clean up the world's oceans (or even your neighborhood) overnight. It's not reasonable to expect you to improve the nation's schools all by yourself.

Heroism is a fine thing, and it makes good media copy, but if you're really interested in making a genuine contribution, the virtues that will serve you best are perseverance, patience, and cooperation. All that you can reasonably expect to accomplish require these qualities. You have to hang in there and keep doing your bit regularly, sometimes for quite a while, before you see results. And while it's possible for you to do something by yourself, it's usually much more useful to work together with others. If you gather a small but dedicated group and you each do a little bit every day or every week, and you keep on doing it for a while, you might be surprised at the results. In time, your idea of what you can reasonably do, your expectations of yourself, and your estimation of your abilities will expand as you see for yourself how much you can accomplish by just keeping at it.

The flip side of what you can expect is what can be expected of you. Different projects require different levels of commitment. Many activities involve hospitals, environmental organizations, senior homes, and other agencies and institutions, which have volunteer-services specialists. These people can give you the knowledge and skills you need to make a real difference, but they need to know they can count on you to complete your full term of service, however long or short that may be. The greater the effect you want to have, the greater your commitment needs to be.

But even if you don't feel able or willing to dedicate lots of time to community service, you can still do something meaningful within your "commitment budget." That's why this book includes a wide variety of projects, some fairly quick and easy, and some that take a while to accomplish. Some can be done by just one or two people, and some require help from many different kinds of people and organizations. So pick a project you think is important and figure out what you can do. Chapter 2 gives you some pointers for choosing a service project that will make you an even more important member of your community.

2

Taking

Action

A vision without a task is but a dream
A task without a vision is drudgery
A task and a vision together is the hope of the world.
— Found on a church wall in Essex, England, 1700

Creating Our Future

Like you, many young people realize that the world they're about to inherit has some serious problems. They may not know what they can do to help, or perhaps they don't believe anything they can do will make a difference. This is not the case. There are many things you can do, both big and small, and our interconnectedness with communities everywhere guarantees an effect.

You may find that the best way to begin community service is to choose a short-term or even one-time project, something fairly small and simple just to get the hang of it, and take on more complex projects as you go along. But if you want to tackle something bigger, go right ahead. What matters is that you realize that you have the ability and the right to shape your future. It's important that you learn how to take an active part in designing the kind of world you want to live in. Once you have a vision of the future, it's up to you to help create it.

Steps for Community Service and Social Action

This book gives you many suggestions for serving your community, country, and planet, but ultimately you know your neighborhood best—its needs, people, resources, and potential. Therefore, use this section not only to choose, plan, and carry out the projects described in this book, but also to create community-service and social-change projects of your own. You know better than any book what your specific locale offers that allows you to "think globally and act locally," as the saying goes. How you elect to serve is up to you.

Choose an Issue

Think about things that can be improved in your community, while keeping in mind the broad definition of this word, and ask yourself the following questions:

What Does Your Community Need?   Look around you. What don't you like about your community (however you choose to define it)? What needs fixing, cleaning, or improving? Is there a lot of trash in the streets? Are there people who could use some help, such as the elderly or the homeless or the sick? Who seems needy or unhappy? What's ugly, bothersome, or unjust? Think about this for a while and make a list. As you go about your daily life, keep your eyes and ears open for things that need improvement, and add them to your list.

At this point, the sky's the limit. Write down *everything* you'd like to do something about, no matter how big or how small, how easy or how complicated. Once you have a fairly long list, you can start narrowing it down, but hold onto the original list. As you acquire skills and experience, you'll be able to tackle some of the bigger items on your list.

What Seems Reasonable for You to Do?   Look over your list. It will probably include some things that are too big and complicated to tackle right now (but again, don't erase them—keep them for later). There might also be some things that seem too big but perhaps can be scaled down. For example, if you have "world hunger" on your list, try to bring it down to size by looking at *local* hunger. You may not be able to feed the world, but maybe you can feed some hungry people in your town. If you think peace is important and you'd like to do something to promote it, you don't have to jet around the world stopping wars; you can look at sources of conflict in your own community and work to resolve them.

Many big problems are cumulative, the sum total of several smaller problems, so break things down and look at the local picture. If you feed people in your own town, you really are helping world hunger: Aren't you and these people part of the world? You can help the big, worldwide problems in small, local ways. And every little bit counts.

What Are You Most Interested In?   Now you've got a smaller list of projects you can reasonably expect to accomplish. But you still have to narrow it down to one particular project. Of all these projects, which one interests you the most? Interest is important, because it keeps you motivated. It's much easier to devote the necessary time and effort to a project you care about.

Do Your Research

Find out all you can about the issue that most interests you. The more you know about it, the better your chances of success are. For example, if you're concerned about litter in your neighborhood, examine the litter to determine what kinds of things are being tossed—candy wrappers, food containers, packaging materials, newspapers, and so forth. If you find that most of the litter is, say, fast-food wrappers, you may want to concentrate on eliminating these items. Find out how many trash cans there are in your area and where they're located. Contact your local waste-disposal department and other government agencies for information. You may want to contact the fast-food places themselves and see if they'll work with you on solving the problem.

If you're worried about air pollution, read books and articles about it. Contact government and private agencies. Check the resources listed in this book, your library, and the phone book for organizations that know about air pollution. Gather all the information you can.

Find out how others in your community feel about your issue, whatever it may be. Conduct an informal survey: Write a questionnaire and get as many people (and as many *kinds* of people—young, old, black, white, and so forth) as you can to answer it, and analyze the results. Find out how officials feel about the issue and what they're doing about it. Write letters to people or organizations for information. Read magazines and newspapers. Check out videos and books from the library. Inform yourself.

Brainstorm

Get a group of concerned people together and see how many solutions you can come up with. Don't reject any ideas at this point, no matter how weird or silly they may seem. Creative solutions require creative thinking, and creative thinking requires a free flow of ideas. Besides, sometimes the weirdest ideas turn out to be the best. Write down all the ideas generated in this session.

Select a Solution

Go through your list of ideas and discuss each one. Try to determine what materials, personnel, and kinds of work are required to carry out each idea. Ask such questions as: How many people do we need for this project? When and where can we do it? How long will it take? What materials, equipment, and services do we need, and how can we get them? Narrow your list down to one or two ideas that are feasible, given your resources and abilities, without underestimating yourself.

Devise a Plan

These are some of the questions you need to ask in formulating a good plan:

❏ What materials and equipment do you need? What can you make yourself, what can you borrow or solicit as donations, and what will you have to buy?

❏ Whose assistance, permission, or cooperation do you need—for example, government officials, professionals, workers, media?

❏ Who is likely to oppose your plan? How much of an effect is this opposition likely to have? What can you do to counteract it?

❏ How much time do you have? When do you start? When do you finish?

❏ What tasks need to be done—writing letters, getting materials, mailing, cleaning up, going door to door, and so forth? Who will do these tasks?

❏ How many people do you need, and how will you get them to help?

❏ What particular skills do you need, and how do you get people with those skills, if you don't already have them?

❏ Will you need money? How much? How will you get it?

❏ If you need to make calls or write letters, what will you say?

You'll probably come up with other questions. Try to think of as many details as possible, cover all your bases, and be as specific as possible. For example, if you say, "We need to get trash bags," think of where you can get them and who'll be responsible for getting them. Be fussy about details. It may seem nitpicky, but it will save you a lot of time and trouble in the long run. If you can't answer a lot of these questions, or the answers are too vague or daunting to be useful, you may want to choose a different project.

Basically, your plan will address what you need to do; how, when, and where you will do it; and who will do what. Make a list of all the steps you need to take and who will do each step. Write it down and distribute it so that everyone knows exactly what's happening and what they need to do.

Get Support

If you need more people, use publicity and other means of persuasion (some of the books in the resource section can help you with this, as well as some of the pointers in Chapter 8) to recruit people who are aware of the problem and agree with your approach to solving it. Let them know what you're doing and how they can help. If your plan is in writing, people can see exactly what you have in mind and more easily envision themselves getting involved, and your requests will be taken more seriously.

Carry On!

You have a plan, you have people, you have materials—now do it!

Evaluate: Learn from Your Mistakes

Unless you are a superhuman genius with supernatural abilities, you will make mistakes. It's inevitable. This isn't a bad thing—it's the way we learn. Mistakes aren't failures; they're a way of finding out what we need to know and what skills we need to acquire. What's important is not to give up, but to learn from your mistakes.

When a project is over, or you hit a snag and aren't sure how to carry on, stop and examine how well (or not so well) you're doing: What has worked well? What hasn't worked well? Try to be very specific. It doesn't help to say, "The project didn't work," or "The project went very well." The project didn't happen all at once—it occurred in parts or stages: First you did this, then you did that, then you did this other thing. Look at the different parts, and determine what worked and what didn't. Why did some things work while others didn't? Should some things be changed? What can be improved? Whom can you ask for help? Are your expectations realistic? Remember that nothing works 100 percent all the time, and things rarely turn out exactly the way we think they will, especially the first time we do something new. Be prepared for surprises, both pleasant and unpleasant.

Can you learn from what you did right to improve your overall results the next time around? Did you have everything you needed? Did you do everything you needed to do? Sometimes you don't realize what's missing until a project is completed. Maybe you didn't accomplish exactly what you set out to do, but you've learned something about how to accomplish it. You have knowledge and skills you didn't have before. Now you can try it again, this time using your new knowledge and skills.

Be flexible, optimistic, patient, and persistent. Improve things that don't work well, or discard them if they can't be fixed. Keep trying until you find the best way. Don't get discouraged, and don't let others discourage you.

Let People Know

Don't be shy about letting others in your community know about your service activities, by word of mouth, displays, flyers, or news releases (see Chapter 8). Not only does this help ensure that credit is given where it is due; it also raises awareness of the cause your group is serving, which may inspire others to perform some sort of service themselves or help you with your efforts.

3

The Sick,

The Needy, and

The Elderly:

Hospitals, Shelters,

and Homes

"When I was in the hospital for surgery," states Connie, a cancer survivor, "I was lucky to have many friends and family members around to visit me and let me know they cared. I knew I was going to be fine, thanks in part to the support and affection of my friends and family." Today Connie has been cancer-free for 40 years.

You've probably been sick yourself at some point, whether it was a case of the flu or a serious illness requiring hospitalization. Try to remember what it was like, how lousy you felt, and how much a little TLC helped—a card, a visit, a bowl of chicken soup, a good laugh—anything that took your mind off your troubles and made you feel cared for. Loving attention, it has been suggested, helps people heal more quickly.

Sick people in hospitals, homeless people in shelters, elderly people in homes for the aged—all these people are *institutionalized*; that is, in a place, or dependent on an agency or organization, that provides medical care or somewhere to live or sleep. Such institutions can include:

- Children's hospitals and clinics
- Senior-citizen residences
- Nursing homes
- Convalescent hospitals and homes
- Veterans' homes and hospitals
- Homeless, women's, and runaway shelters
- Mental institutions and halfway houses
- Hospitals and hospices
- AIDS clinics and support services
- Other places and organizations that provide care for needy, sick, disabled, elderly, or otherwise unfortunate children and adults.

These people and the organizations that serve them can use some help, from a little cheering up to clerical work to donations. The projects in this chapter are intended to help you locate opportunities for providing much-needed attention to the sick, the needy, and the elderly.

Before You Plan Anything: Working with Institutions

Most institutions and support organizations have a department (or at least a person) to supervise and assist volunteers. Usually it's called the Volunteer Services Department or something similar, while an individual may be called the Volunteer Coordinator. These people can let you know what kind of help they need most and the best way to go about assisting them, which saves you a lot of time and trouble. Before you do anything (or get too far in your plans) for any kind of institution, contact the Volunteer Services Department (or person) and tell them what you have in mind.

In addition to the activities described in this book, the volunteer-services people may have some ideas or projects of their own in which you can get involved. Ask them what they need and what has worked well in the past. There also may be organizations that specialize in serving institutionalized or homebound people of different kinds in your area, in which case you might want to work with them instead of on your own.

Finding the Right Institution

If you know the name of the place where you want to work, check the phone book or directory assistance. If you don't have a particular place in mind and you're just interested in helping, say, a homeless shelter or senior home, there are several ways you can find an appropriate place. The listings at the back of this book include some national numbers and hotlines, which can refer you to organizations and institutions in your area.

Aside from national referrals, your first resource for finding service agencies in your area is the phone book. Check the Yellow Pages under "Hospitals," "Clinics," "Senior Residences," or what-ever heading is appropriate for your project. For homeless, women's, and runaway shelters, as well as government-run hospitals and clin-

Volunteering in Hospitals: Tips and Information

❏ Some hospitals have minimum age limits for those serving in the hospital, usually 14 or 16. But this doesn't mean younger folks can't help out with donations, decorations, gifts, cards, and so on. (It also leaves plenty of other institutions where younger volunteers can be of service, such as rest homes, shelters, hospices, and so forth.)

❏ Young people who meet the age requirement have the opportunity to work anywhere in the hospital: selling at the gift shop, giving out information in the lobby, driving patients to and from home, transporting documents and lab samples, helping with clerical work, and performing other kinds of patient services.

❏ Volunteering at a hospital gives you a chance to see a side of the hospital world you might otherwise never get to see.

❏ A term of community service at a hospital is great way to meet other people your age who share your interests.

❏ Most hospitals hold regular (weekly or monthly) information meetings for people who want to volunteer.

❏ Hospitals love having young people volunteer, since they help create a friendly, cheering environment.

❏ Some hospitals have a student or youth coordinator to encourage and assist young volunteers.

❏ Becoming a hospital volunteer is not to be taken lightly. It's a process; you can't just call up and start the next day. It requires screening, training, and responsibility; you get to learn while you help out.

❏ A term of community service at a hospital (or other institution) looks very good on college applications and resumes.

—From the Volunteer Department at Alta Bates Medical Center, Berkeley, California.

ics, check the government and community-services listings in the front part of the White Pages. There are separate listings for city, county, state, and federal agencies, so even though these pages can be a bit confusing, don't give up. Keep looking and calling.

The names and titles of the various services and departments may vary from place to place, but some key listings might include:

- ❏ AIDS Services
- ❏ Children's Services
- ❏ Disabled Services
- ❏ Family Services
- ❏ Foster Care
- ❏ Health Services
- ❏ Health and Human Services (or just Human Services)
- ❏ Homeless Services
- ❏ Mental Health Services
- ❏ Senior Citizens (or Senior Centers, Senior Services)
- ❏ Veterans
- ❏ Victim Assistance
- ❏ Welfare
- ❏ Youth Services

If none of these headings seems to work, an invaluable resource is the reference desk at your local public library. Call them or drop by and tell them what you're looking for. If they can't give you the exact number of the exact place you're seeking, they'll probably know where you can find it. They have directories and books of information about almost anything you can think of, available to everyone free of charge. (You probably can't take reference books home, so be prepared to copy any information you need, either by hand or by photocopying, in which case you'll need to bring change for the photocopy machine.)

Once you have the number, call the place and ask for the volunteer-services department or coordinator. Before you actually call, make sure you know exactly what you're going to ask. You may even want to write it down, so when someone answers your call, you don't find yourself stammering and groping for words. It saves time (not to mention your pride) if you've got your questions right at your fingertips.

Do the Right Thing

Hospitals and other institutions have rules you may not know about, such as who's allowed to see patients, what kinds of food or activities are best for them. Rules that apply to one place may not apply at another. For example, if you're going to make presents for a children's hospital, make sure the gifts are not so small that the younger children might choke on them. Making peanut brittle or saltwater taffy for a senior home might sound like a good idea until you think about trying to eat these treats with dentures. Projects and gifts that would be fine for one kind of place might not be appropriate or safe for another. Make sure your project doesn't violate any of these rules or policies, as well as the dictates of common sense and good taste.

Projects and Activities

Tray Favors, Centerpieces, and Other Mealtime Decorations

You can make decorations for meal trays, "designer" napkin rings, or table decorations for shelters, hospitals, hospices, nursing homes, or senior homes: paper flowers, shamrocks, hearts, and so forth, depending on the occasion. Decorative items can be as simple or as elaborate as you want, depending on your time, abilities, and resources. Attach a little note or ribbon reading "Compliments of [name of your group]," or something along those lines. Here are some ideas for things to make or use as decorations:

❑ Paper or real flowers, individually or in bouquets
❑ Shamrocks or leprechaun hats for St. Patrick's Day
❑ Hearts for Valentine's Day
❑ Bottle-cap faces: pumpkin faces for Halloween, Santa Clauses or snowmen for Christmas, turkeys or pilgrims for Thanksgiving, Uncle Sams for Fourth of July, bunnies for Easter, happy and/or funny faces year-round
❑ Paper-mache or cloth figures or dolls
❑ Get-well or other greeting cards
❑ Place mats with holiday or seasonal themes
❑ Flowers or plants, donated from florists or people's gardens, or bought.

Once the items are made, follow the delivery instructions you received from the volunteer coordinator at the institution. The resource section in Chapter 9 lists some arts and crafts organizations and publications for ideas and instructions. Also see Chapter 4 on holidays.

Decorations and Artwork

Hospitals and homes try to make their surroundings as cheerful as possible for their patients or residents, and decorations are always in demand. You can make decorations and send or deliver them to the hospital or home, or deliver them and help to put them up, depending on what the institution prefers. The decorations don't need to be fancy—just bright and cheerful.

For seasons, make paper flowers, leaves, snowflakes, raindrops, fruit, and so forth. Colorful paper chains, flowers, leaves, pictures, and other all-purpose decorations are good for any time of the year, so the hospital or home doesn't find itself bare and drab between holidays. Some more ideas are:

- ❏ Candles, real or artificial
- ❏ Wreaths made of holly, maize, flowers, pine cones and boughs, leaves, and so forth
- ❏ Banners and flags
- ❏ Posters, collages, sculptures, and other artwork

The sky's the limit, so use your imagination!

Corsages and Accessories for All Occasions

You can make corsages of many different kinds of materials for all kinds of occasions. For Christmas you can make bright corsages of jingling bells or other ornaments, holly, and ribbons. For Valentine's Day, use hearts, flowers, and colored ribbons. A St. Patrick's Day corsage can be made of shamrocks and green ribbons. Use little brooms, bats, red and orange leaves, and black and orange ribbons for Halloween corsages. All-occasion or seasonal corsages can be constructed of such materials as tiny pine cones, dried flowers, shells, beads, bells, ribbons, yarn, bows, and many other objects and trinkets. If people at the hospital or home don't want you to use sharp pins, make bracelet corsages that can be tied around the wrist with a ribbon.

Of course, you're not limited to corsages. You can make all kinds of hand-crafted accessories: beadwork and jewelry, leatherwork, sachets, needlework, and much more.

Gift Boxes

Many occasions celebrated in institutions—birthdays, Christmas, Hanukkah, and so forth—involve giving gifts. Sometimes senior homes and other institutions celebrate a "monthly birthday," in which everyone who has a birthday during that month is honored at one big party. It takes a lot of boxes and wrapping paper to contain the gifts, so some places like to use prewrapped (and often reusable) boxes. Wrapped shoe boxes work very well for this purpose. The tops and bottoms of the boxes are wrapped separately, so that gifts can be popped in and the box tied with ribbon.

One of your local hospitals, senior homes, or other institutions may need some prewrapped gift boxes. If so, check with local shoe stores to supply the boxes, and stationery and party-supply stores to donate the paper, tape, scissors, and so forth. (See Chapter 8 for tips on getting businesses to help.) Then have a wrapping party: Gather all your materials, rent a video, get some dry snacks (greasy fingerprints on the paper will ruin your project), and wrap the boxes and the box tops (separately). Follow instructions from the volunteer people at your targeted institution in delivering the finished product.

Baby Clothes and Blankets

When new parents can't afford clothing for their baby, some hospitals supply them with baby clothes. There are also many babies living in women's and homeless shelters, as well as orphan or foster babies, who can use extra clothing and blankets. You can donate baby clothes and blankets to needy new parents, shelters, or medical clinics. Contact such places to find out what they need.

You can provide all the donated items or conduct a collection drive (see Chapter 8 for directions). As always, follow the instructions from the hospital or shelter for delivery (see the section on women's shelters in this chapter for additional information).

A youth club in the Midwest became involved in a project of this kind by making baby blankets and quilts decorated with their club's logo. One of the adult volunteers who worked with the club also served as an emergency foster parent, caring for babies and small children for a few days until the agency found permanent caretakers. Once when she was asked to care for a baby over the weekend, she was pleasantly surprised to see the baby arrive wrapped in one of her club's blankets!

Scrapbooks and Happy Pills

Collect cartoons, jokes, and funny articles and put them together in attractive scrapbooks for libraries, common rooms, and waiting rooms at hospitals and convalescent homes.

One children's group created a variation on this theme: They inserted each clipping into an oversized gelatin capsule. The capsules were bottled and labeled "Happy Pills," and the bottles were placed in the library, day rooms, and other social areas of local hospitals. Patients or visitors who wanted a laugh could take out a capsule, look at the joke, and put it back in the bottle for the next user.

Whatever you choose to do, package it so that it is fairly durable and can be used again and again, and make it cheerful and attractive. Be sure to let people know who's responsible—that's part of the appeal. If you make a scrapbook, the title page should give credit where credit is due: For example, "This book was written, illustrated, and produced by [your group]," or name yourself if you are the sole author. Each "Happy Pills" jar should also have a credit on it. You should also include a credit line indicating the sources of your jokes and stories.

As always, clear plans ahead of time with the home or hospital staff, and follow the guidelines they give you.

How to Make a Baby Blanket

You'll need:

❑ A sewing machine: If you don't have access to one, either at home or through a friend or relative, you may be able to use a machine at your (or another) school. If you don't know how to use a sewing machine, be sure to get thorough instructions before attempting to use one. It's possible to sew the blanket by hand, but it's much faster and easier with a machine.

❑ About 1½ yards of flannel or pre-quilted cotton, available at fabric stores. Most fabric is sold in widths of either 44 or 60 inches; you need a 44-inch width. Retail prices are $6–$8 per yard, but if you can get remnants, it will be much cheaper. You may even be able to persuade the store to donate all or part of the materials (see Chapter 8).

❑ Two packets of cotton, double-folded seam binding: This goes around the edges of the blanket. Choose the color to match or contrast with the blanket fabric. This costs about $1.50 per packet, and once again, you may be able to have it donated.

❑ A spool of thread that matches the binding color

❑ Straight pins (at least 50)

❑ Scissors.

Instructions:

1. Wash and dry the fabric (and iron it if needed) so it's preshrunk and won't warp or shrink later.

2. Tuck the seam binding around the edges of the fabric so that no edges show, neither on the binding nor on the fabric, like the trimmed edges

Outings with Institutionalized Seniors or Children

Arrange with a senior home or children's group for a day's outing—a picnic, barbecue, day at the beach, bowling or skating party, nature walk, cookie-making day, trip to a museum or park, or other activity that's suitable for the age and strength of the guests. It's probably not a good idea to take frail seniors ice skating, for example, or hyperactive children to the symphony.

of a regular blanket. Pin it in place as you go along, setting the pins perpendicular to the border. It's preferable to use a single long piece of binding that goes all the way around the blanket, but if this isn't possible, use two overlapping pieces. What's important is that the binding goes all the way around the edges evenly and neatly, with no gaps.

3. When cutting anything, remember the old builder's adage: measure twice, cut once. In other words, measure carefully at least twice before doing anything irreversible like cutting.

4. Pin the binding neatly and securely, holding it firmly in place to be sewn. Once it's pinned, check all around and on both sides for any mishaps—warps, gaps, bunching, and so forth—and correct them before sewing.

5. The actual sewing is quick and easy, but don't rush: It's harder to repair a badly sewn item than to go slowly and carefully the first time. Run the edges through the machine so that the resulting seam is about ¼ inch from the inside edge of the binding (as it is on a store-bought blanket).

6. Take out the pins, and you've got a nice, soft, cuddly blanket for some deserving baby.

7. For that designer touch (and to let people know who's responsible for such fine work), sew labels with your group's name on them into the corners of the blankets. Use plain, sturdy cloth that won't unravel, no bigger than 3 square inches. If you write the name on the label (as opposed to, say, embroidering it), be sure to use a permanent ink that won't run after the blanket is washed.

This project will take some planning. You'll have to arrange time, place, scheduling, transportation, materials and equipment, and other critical matters. Coordinate closely with the institution on every aspect of the trip. They're responsible for their patients or residents, so they'll want to have all the details: Where are you going? What day and time? How will you get there? How many people are there in your group to supervise the outing? What supplies are you providing? Is your destination wheelchair accessible; does it have a lot of stairs? Is there drinking water for taking medications?

Sometimes the health center can help out with some of the arrangements. For example, if you need transportation, the center may have vans you can use. If transportation is unavailable, what's within walking distance?

If you're doing a picnic or other "eating out" event, you have to bring food, drink, and cooking equipment (for example, a spatula and charcoal). Make sure it's okay to cook where you plan to go. For example, if you're planning a hot dog roast on the beach, contact the Parks and Recreation Department (or whoever is in charge of the beach) to see if it's all right to barbecue on the beach. Having a park ranger put out your fire is sure to put a damper on your day, and raw franks just aren't as festive!

If you're going to a museum, skating rink, or some other educational or recreational facility, make sure it's open at the time you want to go, and that your plans will not violate any of their rules or policies. Call the facility beforehand and make sure what you have planned is okay with them. Again, it would be disastrous to arrive at the planetarium with 25 children all set for star-gazing, only to find out it doesn't accommodate groups larger than 20.

Planning the logistics of an outing takes some work, but there's nothing mysterious about it—it just has to be done. It might be a good idea to talk to a teacher at your school who has experience with organizing field trips for some more pointers.

Parties for Patients or Residents

Everyone loves a party, and people in institutions are no exception. You may want to choose a time between holidays, since many institutions already provide holiday activities.

As with outings (see above), you need to work closely with the institution's staff to make this happen. They will undoubtedly have guidelines you'll need to follow, and they'll want specific, detailed information about your plans.

It may be possible to include the patients or residents in the planning process. You can divide into committees for planning, activities and entertainment, refreshments, and decorations. Your group and the seniors (or children or whoever is involved) can share responsibilities in some reasonable way. Or you can do it all yourselves.

Discuss the party with the residents and staff to decide on a good time and date, and sketch out a rough menu and program. Then make a list of everything that has to be done—acquire and bring food and drink, make and put up decorations, bring games, arrange for music (live or taped), and so forth—and make sure each and every detail is assigned. (See the box in Chapter 4 for some party tips.)

On the day of the party, arrive early to set up, stay late to clean up, and be a good host (you're throwing the party) and a good guest (it's their place).

Movie Parties

We all need a good laugh, cry, or thrill now and again, and the safest, easiest way of getting one is with a movie. For a movie party with patients or residents of a home, hospital, or other institution, you'll need:

❑ A specific time and place
❑ A working VCR and monitor (TV)
❑ A movie on videotape
❑ Enough seating and space so everyone can see comfortably
❑ Clearance of all plans with the institution's staff and residents.

If the institution doesn't have a VCR, perhaps some parents can loan theirs. Many video-rental outlets also rent VCRs; you may be able to persuade the rental store to give you a discount or donate the VCR and tape, since it's for a charitable cause (see Chapter 8). Arrange the date, time, and place with the institution, and if you're renting a VCR, make sure there's a television monitor available and someone who knows how to hook the VCR up. Take a vote among your group and patients or residents to decide on a movie everyone would like to see. If possible, serve popcorn, sodas, hot dogs, and other traditional snacks, as well as some healthier alternatives like fruit, juice, trail mix, and so forth.

Recreational and Other Equipment for Institutions

Contact a local senior home, hospital, or children's institution to see what they need. Then start a fund (see Chapter 8 for details) to buy toys, games, books, and other entertainment items, or have a collection drive and obtain the items themselves.

That's Entertainment!

Develop an adaptable program of skits, songs, raps, dances, puppet shows, magic acts, recitations, and so forth, to present as a show at hospitals, senior homes, special-education schools, nursing homes, and the like. Then take your show on the road. Your repertoire can include anything from stand-up to Shakespeare, rap to Mozart. It should run at least half an hour or as long as one hour—long enough to be entertaining, but not so long that it will wear out your audience. Length will vary depending on the audience: Sick people tire easily, and children have shorter attention spans, but seniors can handle more. Keep it varied and fairly light: This is not the time to explore existential dilemmas or polish that scene from Kafka.

With your group, make a list of what kinds of acts you are able and willing to do. Who can sing, juggle, dance? Who does magic? Who plays an instrument? Who likes to act, tell jokes, lip sync? In short, what talents do you have at your disposal? (You probably have more than you think, once you get warmed up.) Once you have an idea of the talents and skills you share among you, develop a program list.

To develop a sharp act, get some help from your school's drama department, or from a nearby college or theater company. These companies can also help with costumes, props, sets, and other performance apparatus, which should be minimal, since you want to keep things as portable as possible. If you're asking help from your (or another) school, find out who's in charge of the drama department, and call him or her to discuss what you have in mind. A college theater department can be reached by calling the school's main switchboard number (get it from the phone book or directory assistance). Then the switchboard will connect you with the theater department. Ask to speak to the head of the department, but be prepared to be referred to someone else.

For a theater company, look in the Yellow Pages under "Theater Companies" (or some variation of that) and follow roughly the same procedure, except that you'll need to ask for the community-relations coordinator instead of the head of the department. Follow the guidelines in Chapter 8 for getting people to help out.

Help for Children in Foster Homes, Orphanages, and Other Institutions

Children who have been placed in foster homes, orphanages, or other facilities and/or have been taken from their parents' custody experience the world as a scary place. These children need a lot of reassurance that someone cares about them. Contact your local child-placement agency (check "Foster Care" or a similar listing) to find out what the children might need or want the most.

As a rule, orphanages are not in use anymore; most children waiting for adoption are placed in foster homes, either on a short-term or long-term basis. Some older children live in group homes. The arrangements vary from county to county, so contact the authorities before you make any detailed plans.

The rules and regulations surrounding children in foster care or in the care of the state are quite rigorous and vary widely from state to state. Be aware that confidentiality requirements and bureaucratic restrictions may limit participation opportunities. Your best bet for helping foster children and teens is through the official foster-care agencies. The most effective way would probably be to work with a nongovernmental community organization that provides and supports services for children, including foster-care agencies and many other kinds of programs.

In the San Francisco area, for example, foster-care and other child-serving agencies receive a great deal of assistance from two community programs: Cherish Our Children, sponsored by a local TV station, and Season of Sharing, a charitable program that operates through a major newspaper. They do most of their business around the winter holidays, but the proceeds often carry them through the whole year. For instance, the holiday donations from one Season of Sharing enabled the agency to send dozens of children to summer camp that year. These community-based programs are outside the government bureaucracy and therefore are not subject to the same restrictions. They're open to community participation, and the money they collect can be used more freely.

Your local foster-care agencies will probably be more than happy to help you get in touch with such programs. Another route to consider is contacting the Children's Defense Fund and other national organizations (see resource listings in Chapter 9) to inquire about programs and organizations in your area.

Visits

More than decorations or new clothes or entertainment, often more than money, people crave meaningful contact with other people; for someone who's sick or homeless or has trouble getting out and about, loneliness can be as much of a problem as physical illness. Just a visit to chat and play cards or read can really make a difference. A regular visit—say, once or twice a month—can be the beginning of a valuable friendship and can benefit you as well as the person you're visiting. The more consistent you are, the better. Regular visits can help to establish a meaningful friendship.

There are national organizations that specialize in setting up visits between young people and seniors, such as Magic Me (see the resource listings in Chapter 9). There may also be organizations in your area that facilitate visits to elders, the sick, and others in need of comfort and company. Check your phone book and other resources mentioned at the beginning of this chapter. Try listings in the phone book, such as "Senior Services" and "Health Department," as well as such programs as Meals on Wheels and local AIDS support-service programs. To locate programs and organizations in your area, contact the CDC's national

AIDS hotline or the Elder Care Locator service; see the resource listings at the end of the book for contact information.

Hospices

Hospices provide care for the dying and support for their families. Providing this type of service may seem depressing, but it can actually be quite uplifting. Many people who have benefited from a hospice remain very grateful and eager to help others in the same situation, and they can be very inspiring to work with. In fact, a hospice in northern Virginia reported a waiting list of people wanting to volunteer. But don't get the idea that they don't need your services, especially if you have some personal experience with a loss of this kind. There's always something you can do.

Young people can help hospices in several ways. In what is sometimes called respite aid, someone goes to the patient's home to give the main caregiver a little time off. While this service is usually performed by a legal adult, there may be opportunities for experienced, responsible, older teens to provide respite, or for anyone to act as an assistant to the respite giver. Some hospices run thrift shops or do some other form of fund-raising, and these efforts can usually use help in staffing and donations. The most common way in which young people help hospices is by doing administrative work—filing, stuffing envelopes, and other "unglamorous" but necessary services.

Last but by no means least, many hospices have youth programs to help children and teens who are grieving for a friend or relative. Anyone who has ever lost a friend or family member knows how painful it is and can offer valuable support and sympathy to someone suffering from a similar loss. There are often support groups and follow-up services in which a young person who has been through it can make a big difference in someone's life. Hospices often offer training for young people in some form of grief assistance, and in return they expect a certain degree of commitment.

Look in the Yellow Pages under "Hospice," or contact the National Hospice Organization, listed in Chapter 9, to find a hospice in your area.

Homeless Shelters

Homeless shelters tend to receive a lot of attention during the holidays, but the homeless need help year-round. Here are some services to consider:

- ❏ Food donations, usually canned goods and other nonperishable items
- ❏ Food preparation or assistance
- ❏ Clothing, especially warm things for winter and clean underclothes
- ❏ Kitchen, bath, and bed items such as bed linens, blankets, towels, plates, silverware, soap, shampoo, and so forth
- ❏ Tutoring and other rehabilitation assistance
- ❏ Recreational items, such as board games and cards
- ❏ Administrative and clerical assistance
- ❏ Outreach services: for example, locating and helping homeless people on the streets.

As always, contact local shelters and agencies to see what they need most before you plan anything too detailed. See the beginning of this chapter and the resources in Chapter 9 for some tips on finding the place at which you want to volunteer. In addition to these agencies and services, try the Salvation Army—they're always actively involved in helping the homeless.

Women's Shelters

There are many things young people can do to help the women and children in women's shelters. Contact your local women's shelter (see the beginning of this chapter and Chapter 9) to see what you can do. Here are some suggestions:

- ❏ Donate disposable diapers, baby food, formula, baby blankets, and clothing, and other baby and child-care items.
- ❏ Give a party for the children.
- ❏ Set a regular time (say, once every month) to visit the shelter and give the mothers a break by babysitting for a few hours.

❏ Collect and donate blankets, linens, pillows, and towels (cleaned before donating), as well as kitchen and cooking items.

❏ Conduct one of the projects mentioned for people in homes and hospitals: decorations, the sock-and-mitten tree (see Chapter 4), outings, visits, and donations of food, clothing, recreational equipment, toiletries, and health items.

❏ Purchase or solicit gift certificates so the women can buy something they especially want or need.

The general guidelines in Chapter 8 for collecting and donating items all apply here: Items should be clean, sorted, usable, and so forth. The shelter may also have specific guidelines of its own. For example, many shelters will not accept any but the softest, most harmless toys; nothing hard, small, or detachable is allowed, for the children's protection. Toy weapons are discouraged, because these children may have a hard enough time learning social and coping skills without being encouraged to play violently.

Security can be rigorous at women's shelters, so don't be surprised if the people in charge refuse to tell you where the shelter is located, which will limit your options. Some of the women are trying to get away from abusive situations, and the shelter makes sure the women are safe by not letting others know where they are. So you may need to restrict your activities to donations of some kind. However you are able to help, it's appreciated.

Runaway Shelters

Homes and shelters for runaways can use the same kind of help as women's and homeless shelters. Check the "Community Service" listings in the phone book. Organizations such as Covenant House, the National Network of Runaway and Youth Services, and Youth Development, Inc. may have facilities in your area (see service and volunteer resources for contact information), or they may know how to get in touch with local runaway and youth services.

Some of the same security conditions for women's shelters may also apply to runaway shelters. Because some of the children and teenagers are fleeing abusive homes, the contact people may not be willing to divulge the shelter's location.

Electric Fans, Heaters, and Other Supplies for Outpatients

When patients return to their homes after a stay in the hospital, they may be more sensitive to heat and cold than they usually are. A small electric fan in summer or a space heater in winter can contribute a great deal to their comfort. Work with the outpatient and discharge facilities of local hospitals to help in this way. Perhaps it would be possible to help the hospital start a "loan closet" of fans and heaters to lend to the patients.

Patients may need other items at home for a short time to help in their recovery, such as humidifiers, canes, mattress pads, and so forth. These items can also be loaned out. Work closely with hospital volunteer coordinators to arrange the logistics: how to keep track of who has what, how to get an item back if the patient doesn't return it, how to keep inventory lists, where to store the items, and so forth.

Supplies for Free Clinics and Medical Nonprofit Organizations

Free clinics and other nonprofit medical facilities can always use help getting medical and general supplies, especially with the cutbacks in medical care funding and programs. If you want to perform some service in this area, first locate a clinic or other institution that could use your help (see the first few sections of this chapter and the resource listings in Chapter 9), and determine what they need that you can provide. Contact the head nurse at local free clinics, women's and homeless shelters, AIDS organizations, and other medical-service facilities, and ask what supplies (and services) are needed. Then decide how you're going to get these supplies—organizing a collection drive, raising funds to purchase supplies, soliciting donations, and so forth (see Chapter 8).

Doctors and medical schools often receive free samples of medicines and medical supplies, so contact them for help with your project. Of course, some of these supplies are not appropriate for "civilian" handling, but there's always a need for such items as bandages, cotton, disinfectant, aspirin, and the like.

Not all supplies need to be strictly medical; some places may need such items as bed linen, pajamas, or diapers. Some of the supplies needed might be fairly unusual. For example, the American Cancer Society keeps a collection of wigs for chemotherapy patients. Specific maladies have specific (and sometimes unexpected) needs—wheelchairs, canes, prostheses, mattress covers, and many types of clothing, accessories, and equipment. Many specific illnesses are represented by their own national advocacy organizations—muscular dystrophy, cerebral palsy, and diabetes are a few examples. Contact them to find out what's needed.

Equipment for the Disabled

In addition to working through organizations, you may know of some people with disabilities who could use equipment or a particular device. You can raise funds to buy, or in some cases, make this equipment for them: ramps, prostheses, mobility devices of all kinds, and so forth.

One way some people with disabilities keep in touch with the world is by computer. It could be a real boon to help someone acquire a computer, which may require special attachments or devices to be usable. If you are interested in this type of project, contact the Foundation for Technology Assistance (see the resource listings in Chapter 9) for help in raising funds and locating equipment.

Daycare and Childcare Centers

Centers that specialize in daycare or childcare need volunteers to read stories, supervise, play games and make crafts, decorate or renovate centers, or help with administrative work. There are reams of rules and laws regulating every aspect of child care, so don't make any elaborate plans without consulting with the proper authorities beforehand. One way to do this is to contact the National Association for Childcare Resource and Referral Agency (see resource listings in Chapter 9 for details), which can then refer you to the correct agency in your area; it's a two-step process. See also the "Community Service," "Social Services," or "Human Services" listings in the phone book.

Despite the many regulations, it is still possible to be a child-care volunteer. The help is very welcome, and working with children is an especially rewarding form of service, so don't be discouraged by the bureaucracy.

Long-distance Gift Certificates

Many long-distance telephone companies offer gift certificates for long-distance phone calls. This is a useful gift to elderly people with children or relatives living far away, exchange students, or recently arrived immigrants. Contact long-distance carriers (MCI, AT&T, Sprint, Working Assets, and so forth) for details.

Help for the Poor Overseas

There are hundreds of projects going on at any given time aimed at relieving poverty abroad. To help the needy in other countries, it's usually best to work with an established, reputable organization. When researching these organizations, be sure to find out the organization's past accomplishments and how it spends its donations. Be aware that some organizations have hidden agendas: For example, some require that people convert to their religion or sign up with their political party in order to receive goods or care. To get this type of information, contact the National Charities Information Bureau, which publishes *The Wise Giving Guide*, or the Council of Better Business Bureaus, Philanthropic Advisory Service (see Chapter 8).

Most organizations prefer that you donate money, but some will accept clothing, canned foods, and other items. Most also allow you to choose the project and/or region to which you want your donation to go. See the general service section in Chapter 9 for worthy organizations.

Adopt a Person or Family

Perhaps you know of a person or family that could use some help not readily available through the usual channels. For example, perhaps someone in your school needs medical relief, or a family of foreigners needs help navigating life in the United States, or an elderly person in your neigborhood seems lonely and helpless. You and your group can "adopt" this person or persons and take him, her, or them under your wing.

You can do this on your own or as a small group, or make the situation a community concern by getting others in your school or neighborhood involved. The service(s) you provide will vary from situation to situation: They can include raising funds, collecting food and clothing, providing referrals to employment and social-service agencies, translating, running errands, or just keeping someone company. As with any service activity, consult with whomever you intend to serve to make sure your help is useful and welcome, and always respect people's dignity, privacy, and rights.

Exchange Programs

Set up an "exchange" program linking well-to-do families with needy families. This can be done through groups such as the PTA, a church or synagogue, or a social-service agency. These organizations are likely to know of appropriate families and can help you set up the program so that everyone's privacy and dignity are respected. You can also contact The Box Project, which runs "sister family" programs to help needy families (see Chapter 9).

Prisoners

The most common way for citizens to help prisoners is by writing letters, either on a one-time basis or as "pen pals." There are many organizations that arrange mail-exchange programs, such as Prison Pen Pals (see Chapter 9). For safety reasons, it's probably best to work with an established organization.

Help for the Homebound

Many elderly or sick people aren't in institutions, but they may be homebound. For someone who is sick or immobilized—whether he or she is an elderly person with arthritis, someone just out of the hospital, or an AIDS patient—simple tasks can become extremely burdensome. Try to imagine getting your laundry done if you couldn't lift anything. Such people can use some help going places and getting things done. Here are some ways you can help those who may not be in institutions but can still use some help:

❑ Provide transportation—or just company and help with packages—for medical appointments, religious services, shopping, and other outings.
❑ Help out with shopping and chores such as groceries, house cleaning, laundry, pet care, and so forth.
❑ Keep in touch through visits, phone calls, letters, and cards.
❑ Go on walks and outings (movies, restaurants, and the like).
❑ Shovel walks, mow lawns, rake leaves, water gardens, put up storm windows, and generally help keep a home safe and neat.
❑ Help the homebound with forms, taxes, bills, and other business.
❑ Run errands like returning library books and videos, picking up prescriptions, groceries, mail, and so forth.

You and your group can do this on your own, serving folks in your own neighborhood, or you can hook up with a program that does this type of work, such as Meals on Wheels, which delivers hot, home-cooked meals to homebound seniors. Some communities have similar programs for AIDS patients. Contact the National AIDS Hotline or the Elder Care Locator number, listed in Chapter 9, for established programs in your area.

4

Holidays

Have you ever been to a party where everyone but you seemed to be having fun? There's nothing lonelier or more wretched than feeling miserable when everyone around you is having the time of their lives. Everyone else's high spirits just seem to sink yours lower.

Think of what it must be like for a sick child in the hospital or a homeless person in a shelter during Christmas or Thanksgiving, when everyone else is getting presents and going to parties and eating way too much and squabbling with their families. Holidays are supposed to be happy times, but for those who are sick, hungry, or lonely, they can be terribly sad. You can help make someone's holiday the warm, cheerful time it should be—or just send the world a bright, positive message—with one or more of the projects in this chapter, or some of the activities in Chapter 3.

Christmas, Hanukkah, and Kwanzaa

The winter holidays can be particularly hard. The combination of bad weather and constant pressure to be jolly is enough to get anyone down. With this in mind, here are a few suggestions for activities that can make this time of year a bit more cheery for the needy.

Toy Collection Drive

Most towns have a toy collection drive, usually through Toys for Tots (sponsored by the Marines), the mayor's office, or a local charity or civic group. It's best to work with an established toy drive instead of starting one of your own. Well before the holidays (at least a month before), contact the organization in charge of the toy drive to find out the details. If you don't know which organization it is, you can call the social-services department of your city or county. Another idea is to call the community-affairs or public-affairs office of a local television or radio station, since the media usually help publicize toy drives. In addition, watch for posters, flyers, newspaper ads, and radio and TV announcements.

Contact the toy-drive organizers to find out how your group can help—by collecting or helping sort and clean toys, making posters and banners, picking up and delivering toys, or assisting at collection stations. Find out where the collection points are. Your group can do its own mini-collection at school or in the neighborhood and then donate what you've received to the toy drive.

UNICEF Cards

UNICEF, the United Nation Children's Fund, produces beautiful holiday cards that can be sold on consignment. The proceeds go toward services that assist children worldwide. You can sell these cards as a fund-raiser, or buy some yourself to send a bit of holiday cheer to someone who needs it. See the resource listings for UNICEF contact information.

Donate and/or Decorate Trees, Menorahs, or Kwanzaa Displays

Another way to promote holiday cheer is to donate Christmas trees, menorahs and candles, or Kwanzaa candles and corn to shelters, clinics, and other centers. Fire and other regulations prevent some institutions from using certain kinds of displays, so be sure to check with administrators where you wish to donate before buying or making anything. And keep in mind several alternatives: for example, you can buy aluminum trees, or make trees from old umbrella frames, wired upside-down in a stacked effect, and decorate them with fireproof materials. Kwanzaa and Hanukkah candles may have to be electric or otherwise simulated.

Some institutions have trees but not enough ornaments. You can make paper and popcorn chains, and homemade ornaments made of paper, Styrofoam balls, cloth, and so forth. Or you can get a group of people at school or in the neighborhood to each bring one or two ornaments from home to donate. If every student in the school brought one ornament, the hospital (or home or other institution) could probably decorate all its trees and then some. Collect empty ornament boxes, and gather the ornaments from others. A variation on regular tree ornaments is the "sock and mitten" tree (see below), which works well for homeless and/or women's shelters.

You can devise fun and interesting multicultural variations on these holiday decorating ideas, combining elements of Hanukkah, Kwanzaa, and Christmas: a tree hung with corn and Hanukkah gelt (chocolate coins), a menorah with Kwanzaa candles, a mantle hung with stockings and decorated with a Kwanzaa display. Be creative, and try to make sure everyone feels included in your holiday celebrations. But be sure to consult people from the cultures and traditions you want to include to ensure that you are representing them accurately. In addition, check with institutions ahead of time to ensure that no one will take offense at a hybrid holiday display.

Sock and Mitten Tree

Every year, folks at Oakland Children's Hospital set up a large tree in the cafeteria. The tree is then decorated with donated pairs of socks, mittens, and gloves in many different sizes and colors. They are hung on the tree with string or hooks. The final result is very pretty and original-looking, and those patients who are able can help with the decorating. After Christmas, the socks and mittens are given to the patients. A sock and mitten tree would also work in any hospital, senior home, or shelter. Scarves or mufflers could also be added, draped around the tree like garlands.

Children's Hospital also does a variation on this theme for their infants: the "rattle tree." There is always a large demand for rattles for the babies, and this is a good way of gathering them. Contact your local institutions to see if any of these ideas will work for them.

Kwanzaa Cornucopias

In addition to the symbolic corn, your Kwanzaa displays can include pretty and appropriate edibles, such as candy apples, popcorn balls, sweet potato pies, and other goodies. A nice arrangement of these and other treats in a basket or cornucopia make a memorable, useful, and delicious addition to a Kwanzaa display. You can also include African table coverings (e.g., kinte or mud cloth), to be used later as blankets, as well as caps, vests, and all kinds of warm clothing in other traditional fabrics.

Make and/or Fill Stockings

If you plan far in advance, you can usually get ready-made Christmas stockings extremely cheaply or even for free right after the winter holidays, and then save them for the following year. You can then decorate these ready-made stockings with glitter, cotton, felt or other fabric cutouts, or small ornaments.

If you decide to make Christmas stockings, you'll need materials and labor. Here are various options:

- ❏ You can make them yourselves (see box in this chapter).
- ❏ If there's a sewing club or needlework society in your neighborhood or town, contact them to see if they would help you sew the stockings.
- ❏ If your school has a sewing class, contact the teacher of the class and ask if she or he will have students sew them, or if the teacher can show you how and let you use the sewing machine.
- ❏ If your school doesn't have sewing class, contact nearby middle schools, high schools, and vocational schools. Contact the sewing or home-economics teacher to see if that person can help.
- ❏ For help, contact any parents or volunteers who have a sewing machine.

Whichever option you choose, be sure to send a thank-you note or certificate of appreciation to your helpers (see Chapter 8).

You can then decorate the stockings and donate them empty, or you can collect small gifts as stocking stuffers. Types of gifts will depend on your intended recipients. There are many different kinds of toys, sweets, and treats—little books, mittens, barrettes, colorful shoelaces, sachets, cards, fruit, and so forth—that children will be happy to receive. Keep in mind such factors as age and gender.

How to Make a Christmas Stocking

You'll need:
- ❑ About half a yard of red, green, or white thick felt
- ❑ A darning needle (they're big, with big eyes)
- ❑ Yarn colored to match or contrast with the felt
- ❑ Scissors
- ❑ A piece of cardboard cut into the shape of a stocking
- ❑ Chalk.

Instructions:
1. Fold the cloth in half.
2. Place the cardboard stocking on the folded cloth so that the sole of the foot is on the fold, and trace its outline with the chalk.
3. Cut out the stocking shape, keeping the fabric folded at the sole.
4. Thread the darning needle with a double length of yarn: That is, put the yarn through the eye of the needle and pull it through so the ends of the yarn meet, and then tie a small knot at the end. The resulting length should be about two feet of double yarn.
5. Beginning at the top, sew down the sides by poking the needle through the cloth (about ¼ inch from the edge), pulling it all the way through, and poking the needle through again from the same side as before, so you end up sort of wrapping the thread around the seam with your stitch. When you reach the sole of the foot, where the fabric is folded, knot the yarn tightly, cut it, and start on the other side. Keep stitches small (about ¼ or ⅓ inch) and even, so your seam is strong and neat.
6. Add a few extra stitches in the same spot at the beginning and end of each seam for strength. Remember, you'll be putting stuff in the stocking, so make sure it is strong enough to hold items.
7. Turn the stocking inside out or leave the seams showing. Decorate as desired.

For seniors and other adults, you can stuff stockings with such things as combs, toiletries, soap, perfume, cologne, sachets, fruit, sweets (for seniors, avoid anything that's hard to eat with dentures), games and puzzles, playing cards, and other items as indicated by the home or hospital.

For women's shelters, you can combine items for adult women (toiletries, accessories, and so forth) with items for children (rattles, baby food, clothes, toys, and the like). As always, ask the folks at the shelter what is needed and acceptable.

If providing the stockings and/or gifts doesn't work for your situation, then perhaps you can help an organization stuff and distribute its own stockings. Contact local hospitals, shelters, and other institutions to see if they would like a few "Santa's helpers" to stuff stockings or perform other needed tasks.

Wrapping and Labeling Gifts

Some shelters and institutions can use help wrapping and labeling gifts and donations. Usually they ask that you and your group come down to their offices or facilities and be prepared to give them a whole day. About a month before the holidays, contact your local support-services agency, hospital, senior home, or other institution, and ask if they can use your artistic gift-wrapping abilities.

Halloween

Check Chapter 3 for additional ideas you can implement to help others celebrate this holiday.

Halloween Parties

Halloween has become more and more dangerous over the years. You'll be providing a great service to the kids and parents of your community if you create a safe alternative, such as a Halloween party. Get parents and other members of your community involved, by asking them to help decorate the hall, donate refreshments, and

Helping Shelters for Holidays: Tips and Information

❑ **DON'T** serve the homeless and indigent as a form of charitable tourism: "Gee, let's do some project for the homeless so we can see what homeless people are like." They're people, just like you.

❑ **Do** make sure that what you're offering is a real service, not an excuse to observe them like an anthropological experiment.

❑ **Do** respect everyone's rights, dignity, and privacy.

❑ **DON'T** place pressure on the recipient to make a show of gratitude. Allow the person to receive what he or she needs without making a fuss. Anonymous donations are preferable unless a relationship is already established.

❑ **DON'T** undermine parental authority when helping children. Consult parents beforehand—just because someone is sick or homeless doesn't mean that person has lost authority over his or her family.

❑ **Do** call and set up some programs and activities during the year, so that when the holidays roll around, your plans are already made. Even for a one-time project, make contact early, a month or two ahead of time, so your project is as useful and effective as possible.

❑ **DON'T** limit yourself to the winter holidays—people need help all year round, and Valentine's Day, Mother's Day, Veteran's Day, and lots of other holidays are also excellent opportunities for helping the needy.

—Berekeley-Oakland Support Services (BOSS)

organize festivities. See the box below for crucial party considerations. Here are some party ideas:

❑ In one town, the local mall hosted a Halloween party, so children could trick-or-treat safely within the mall. Volunteers, parents, and stores cooperated in setting up booths, games, refreshments, and decorations.

❑ Get a school to sponsor a Halloween party. Parents and volunteers can occupy the classrooms, and children can trick-or-treat around the school. If having Halloween at school seems too dull, try a community center, church, or synagogue.

❏ Go on a hayride.

❏ Set up a Haunted House.

UNICEF

As mentioned in the previous section, UNICEF is a United Nations organization dedicated to helping children all over the world with food, education, medical care, and much more. October 31 is National UNICEF Day, and there are a wide variety of projects in which youth groups can participate:

❏ Food-related activities such as Skip-a-Meal, Share-a-Snack, and dinner parties, which help to feed hungry children at home and abroad

❏ Parties, dances, and pumpkin-carving contests

❏ Adopt-a-Project drives, which raise funds for specific UNICEF projects

❏ The Trick-or-Treat for UNICEF collection drive.

Materials and information for these and more projects are available from UNICEF (see Chapter 9).

Other Halloween Service Activities

Other services you can provide are making environmentally correct trick-or-treat bags for children and serving as chaperones during trick-or-treating or parties. You or your group can set up "Safe Stations" for lost children; publicize your intention in advance, so people know where the stations are. In addition, you can patrol neighborhoods, watching for children's (and others') safety, but it is best to do this with adult supervision.

Questions for a Successful Party

Of course, you already know how to party. But do you know how to *give* a party? This is what you need to consider:

1. How many people can we invite/expect? The answer to this will determine a lot of the other factors.
2. Where will the party be held? The place needs to be big enough to hold everyone, as well as warm, safe, accessible, and affordable.
3. How will we decorate it? Make sure decorations are safe, appropriate, and, well, decorative.
4. What date and time should the party be, and how long should it last? Factors to consider include proximity to Halloween, guests' schedules and bedtimes, and general convenience.
5. What will we have to eat and drink, how much will we need, and how will we get it? Include healthy food along with the usual party fare.
6. What will we do? Appropriate activities need to be planned, materials acquired, and people recruited to run the activities. Keep in mind your guests' ages, attention span, and interests.
7. How will we let people know about it? Flyers, invitations, school notices, posters, word-of-mouth? Timing is critical.
8. How much will this cost? How much stuff and services can we get donated and how much will we actually have to pay for? How will we get the funds we need? (See Chapter 8.)

Other Holidays

Collecting food and clothing for the needy, helping serve food in shelters, visiting people in hospitals and senior homes, and many of the other activities described in this book are appropriate for most holidays. About a month or so before a given holiday, check with local churches, synagogues, hospitals, homes, and shelters to see about any activities or pressing needs. No doubt someone can use your help.

Veterans Day

Many American veterans who fought in World War II, Korea, Vietnam, Desert Storm, and other wars continue to suffer long after the war is over, either from physical wounds or from mental and emotional damage. You can let them know their fellow Americans appreciate their sacrifices.

Check in your phone book for a "Veterans" listing in the government or community-services pages. If there's a veterans' facility near you, call the volunteer-services department to see about visiting them. If there isn't a facility nearby, contact the state or federal Veterans Administration (VA), which can also be found in the phone book, to get addresses for sending cards, gifts, and donations. Your local VA can also suggest other ways you can help.

Another way of showing gratitude and respect to veterans is by taking good care of their graves. This can be a one-time activity—decorating veterans' graves with flowers, flags, and ribbons—or an ongoing project—planting flowers and taking care of them and keeping the graves neat and attractive.

See the chapter about institutionalized people for more suggestions, and remember, you don't have to wait for Veterans Day to show your appreciation for veterans. Contact the facility nearest you to see what's needed (see Chapter 9).

United Nations Day

United Nations Day, October 24, is a good time to remind ourselves of the importance of peace and unity. You can make this day an important holiday in your school or community with peace vigils, refugee assistance, tree plantings, and other service activities with a global outlook. Check the phone book or contact UN headquarters (see resource listings in Chapter 9) to see if your area has a local chapter of the UN Association; perhaps you can participate in some activity they have planned.

Earth Day

Earth Day is April 22. It was first observed in 1970 to draw public attention to the state of our earth, water, and air, and to point out how we can help stop pollution and increase respect for the earth. See Chapter 6 on environmental activities for ways of celebrating Earth Day. For further information, contact the Environmental Protection Agency (see Chapter 9).

Back to School Day

It's not exactly a calendar holiday, but it's certainly a big yearly event in the life of every young person. Collect and/or purchase school supplies for needy children at shelters—pens, pencils, art supplies, notebooks, binders, backpacks, lunch boxes, and the like—so they have what they need for their first day at school.

Other Holidays as Service Opportunities

❑ New Year's Day, January 1: Help your school and community devise some New Year's resolutions for recycling, caring for the needy, and so forth.
❑ Martin Luther King, Jr. Day, third week in January (observance date varies): Emphasize racial unity and learn about various ethnic groups.
❑ Black History Month, February; Lincoln's Birthday, February 12: Focus on justice, equality, and eliminating prejudice.
❑ Valentine's Day, February 14: Through visits, cards, letters, or gifts, there's no better day to "make new friends and keep the old."
❑ February 18: Welcome newcomers to America.
❑ St. Patrick's Day, March 17: Prepare corned beef and cabbage suppers at local shelters or other institutions.

❏ Easter/Passover, late April (exact dates vary): Contact local churches and synagogues to see about service projects in which you can participate.

❏ Mother's Day, second Sunday in May (exact date varies): Throw a party, or send gifts and cards, for mothers in women's and homeless shelters.

❏ Memorial Day, May 30 (observance date varies): Since this day often marks the unofficial beginning of summer, you can distribute information on safe summer fun in your area.

❏ Father's Day, third Sunday in June (exact date varies): Help young fathers become good parents through activities designed to encourage, support, and educate them.

❏ Independence Day, July 4: Help local beaches, parks, and other public gathering places clean up after the fireworks and picnics are over.

❏ Labor Day, September 2: With school just around the corner (or just begun), there's no better time to welcome newcomers with some kind of get-together and perhaps even a guided tour of the school or neighborhood.

❏ Columbus Day/Indigenous People's Day, October 12 (observance date varies): Do research on Native American history and culture; share your new knowledge with others.

5

Schools, Education, and Community

Once upon a time, a junior high-school teacher who shall remain nameless got fed up with the school system (yes, it happens) and asked her students what they would do to improve the schools. Not surprisingly, the students had a lot of good ideas. A few of the ideas and projects in this section come from some of those real-life students—as does some of the inspiration for writing this book.

Along with the projects listed here, you and your friends and classmates probably have some thoughts of your own on the subject; see Chapter 2 for help in developing your ideas. Many of these projects can be done both inside and outside the school, in your neighborhood, apartment complex, and so forth.

Dealing with Bureaucracies

Many of these projects may require a great deal of interaction with bureaucracies: school districts and administrations, city offices, housing authorities, and the like. The dictionary defines a bureaucracy as "government by department officials following an inflexible routine." The key word here is *inflexible*: Schools and city governments tend to be creatures of deeply entrenched habit, and sometimes their methods and ideas are hard to change and not very open to questioning. It may be difficult to persuade bureaucrats to try something new, and some may feel you're encroaching on their territory, so don't be surprised if you meet with a certain amount of resistance. Deal with all opposition with courtesy and tact—and don't give up. Listen carefully to all objections; some of them may be quite valid and may bring up issues you may not have considered. Get help and/or advice from a sympathetic, knowledgeable teacher, parent, or administrator. This recommendation applies to almost every situation, but especially when dealing with bureaucracies.

Projects and Activities

Develop Education Materials for Teachers

What are some (or at least one) of the most memorable, enjoyable, and useful classes and school activities you've had? If you think other students might enjoy them as well, write them down and compile a collection of the best, arranged by grade level and subject. For example, if you had a teacher who used an entertaining, effective way to teach spelling or some other subject, have the teacher write down what he or she did, so you can share it with other teachers, students, and schools.

When you've collected some good lessons, copy them out neatly (on a word processor or typewriter if possible), reproduce them on a photocopier, and bind them into booklets for distribution around the school, district, or neighborhood as a kind of a "Students' Choice" or "Top Ten Lessons." As with any published work, be sure to credit all contributors.

Develop Materials for Students and Others

Create materials for fellow students or neighbors on any number of subjects:

- ❑ **Health.** Drug education, anti-smoking information, AIDS, sports and bike safety, exercise, nutrition, and much more.
- ❑ **The Environment.** Recycling tips, public-transportation information, how to save resources, smart shopping, and more.
- ❑ **Recreation.** Safe, healthy games, toys, places, activities; things that kids and families can do; and more.
- ❑ **Community Service.** Projects and activities your schoolmates and neighbors can do to help others—for example, "Ten Ways You Can Help Our Neighborhood."
- ❑ **Safety and Crime Prevention.** Home-safety tips, self-defense, safe and dangerous places in your school or neighborhood, and so forth.

After choosing a topic, you need to research your subject. Collect as much information as you can find, sort through it for what is most useful and relevant, and write up your findings in a neat, easy-to-use, organized format. It's preferable to use a typewriter or word processor, but if you can't get access to one, copy it out *very neatly* by hand. Illustrations can add to your product's appeal. Then photocopy your materials and, if appropriate, bind them.

The format you choose will depend on how much information you want to impart. You can make (and illustrate) flyers, booklets, pamphlets, fact sheets, or posters on any of this information. The materials can also be in a creative format, like a calendar or coloring book, for instance. Again, give credit where credit is due.

Offer Your Ideas for a Better School or Neighborhood

There are probably a few issues in your school, neighborhood, or town that you and your friends and classmates gripe about regularly. Well, instead of just talking, maybe you can help. Think of ways to improve the things you don't like, and let others know about your ideas. Get together with your friends, classmates, neighbors, and a sympathetic teacher or parent and discuss these problems, and devise some practical, positive solutions.

Write down your ideas clearly and neatly (once again, try to use a typewriter or word processor). Your final draft can be in the form of an appeal ("We ask that all neighbors please use the trash cans . . ." and point out where the trash cans are and why people should use them), a proposal ("We feel that we need more trash cans at more convenient sites . . ." and give specifics of how many, where, and some ideas for getting them), or a simple list ("These are some things we feel can be done to keep our neighborhood cleaner . . ."). Make your appeal, proposal, or list as useful and effective as possible by stating the problem clearly and offering specific solutions. Consider getting help from an English teacher or writer. Then make copies of your proposal or list of ideas and give them to whomever you think needs to see them (ask a reliable adult if you're not sure): the principal, PTA, school board, neighborhood association, students, residents, and so forth.

It's important to keep the emphasis positive: Avoid blaming, accusing, backbiting, or being unkind. These kinds of negative attitudes and behavior invariably make things worse, not better. Treat everyone in the school or neighborhood with respect and courtesy. Don't single out any one person or group. Offer your suggestions in a spirit of positive cooperation and help. Be kind, practical, and generous.

Keep Your School or Neighborhood Clean and Attractive

In addition to being an excellent and often much-needed service, a clean-up and/or maintenance program can help unify a community or school and encourage people to take pride in their community. Here are some ways you can help your school or neighborhood look its best:

❏ Pick up trash.
❏ Make and place trash cans.
❏ Make posters or sponsor a poster contest, with a "Keep Our School (or Neighborhood) Clean" theme.
❏ Fix broken furniture and fixtures (or raise funds to have them fixed).
❏ Clean hallways, grounds, rooms, yards, empty lots: sweep floors, wash walls, erase graffiti, wash windows, pull weeds, cut grass, and so forth.

Contact the school administrators and faculty and the parent-teacher organization for help and for what's needed. For a neighborhood project, contact the neighborhood association, or if there isn't one, a few local leaders: There are usually a few people in the neighborhood who most people know and respect and who set the tone. For public-housing sites, contact the housing authority or site supervisor.

Help for the Library

Helping the school librarian can take the form of shelving books, organizing the card catalog or computer files, making and putting up decorations, repairing books, and so forth. Talk to the librarian to find out what's needed. In public libraries, consult the head librarian or community-affairs office. Many public libraries work with a community group like "Friends of the Library," which would probably know what is needed and how you can help. Here are some suggestions:

Donate Books to the Library. You can buy them or conduct a collection drive. In collecting books, not all your donations will be appropriate for the school library, so perhaps the remaining books can go to a senior home, convalescent home, or hospital. Of course, this project can also be done especially for these kinds of institutions, with children's books going to children's hospitals or homes for the mentally deficient, large-print books to the elderly, or Braille books to the blind. See Chapter 8 for collection-drive guidelines.

Start a Special Section in the Library. Collect and create books, articles, magazines, brochures, posters, models, displays, and other educational materials about a particular topic: ethnic culture (African-, Native-, Chinese-, Irish-, Hispanic-American, and so forth), academic subjects, recreation, local history (see "Oral History" below), health, the environment, countries of the world, space, and much more. Use your imagination, and consider some of the other projects in this chapter for your special section.

Before you do anything, consult with the librarian to make sure there's a space for the collection—shelves, wall space, a tabletop or display site of some sort—and work closely with him or her throughout the project. Design your section when you have a good idea of what materials you have and where the display will go. Let people know who made the display with a sign or plaque.

You can conduct a collection drive to get the materials you need or can't make yourself. Ask stores, museums, colleges, doctors' offices, and other experts for help. In this case, your collection-drive announcements must specify the kinds of items you seek. You may want to consider sending letters or otherwise contacting the people and organizations you need help from or who may have appropriate materials available.

Honor Retiring Teachers

Giving recognition to teachers who have served for a long period of time is a way of calling attention to the contributions they've made. You can honor these individuals by inviting them to a party or ceremony to present gifts or certificates of appreciation. You can also present your gift/certificate at a school assembly or simply leave it in the recipient's box with a card signed by group members. Cards and gifts can be homemade or purchased (or donated).

In a neighborhood setting, this might take the form of honoring local elders, or doing something special for grandparents or mothers or fathers on their appropriate days (Grandparents' Day, Mother's Day, Father's Day).

Apples for Teachers

When was the last time you did something nice for your teacher(s)? Of course, you like some teachers better than others, but all teachers work very hard (probably much harder than you realize), and they don't often get the appreciation they deserve. Appreciation from students themselves is especially meaningful. You can thank your own teachers and the rest of the teachers in the school or district by leaving apples—real or otherwise—in teachers' mailboxes. This can be expanded to a school-wide or district-wide project (coordinate with administrators and/or the PTA), or it can be just for one teacher.

Deliver School Mail

For holidays such as Valentine's Day, Christmas, Hanukkah, and Kwanzaa, deliver cards within the school. This would require coop-eration with the administration and faculty. Make one or more "mailboxes." Announce the service over the PA system, in the school bulletin, with flyers, and so forth, indicating when and where the mailbox(es) will be (good times are before classes and at lunch time in the hallway, the last two days before Christmas vacation, for example). Students and staff can drop their mail in the box(es), which should have attendants.

This service can be free, or you can charge for it and use the money for some other service project, such as blankets for the homeless or food for a food bank. If you decide to charge for it (say, a dime per letter), be sure to point out in your announcements what the money will be used for, and let people know they can donate without mailing a letter. The mailbox attendants can carry canisters to collect the money (see Chapter 8).

Oral History

Chances are that you know people (especially elders) who were present at historic events. They undoubtedly have a wealth of information far more interesting and alive than the accounts given in your history books. If you can think of any people who may have some good stories to tell, interview them and record what they have to say.

When you're finished and if the interviewee agrees, donate your results to the public or school library. This is a wonderful way for people to learn about local and general history—hearing about historical events from an eyewitness or participant is much more immediate than any book could be. And you'll find out what everyday life was like in those historic times, which will give meaning to all of the dates and names you learn in school. The Vietnam and Korean Wars, World War II, Pearl Harbor, the Civil Rights Movement, the Holocaust, the Japanese internment during World War II, Desert Storm, and other important events in recent history can take on a whole new dimension when you hear about them from real people.

You can also compile a history of your town or area in this way. There are probably many people in your own neighborhood who remember what the town was like many years ago. In addition to providing a personalized history of the town, it also gives older people a chance to share some of their memories and experiences. Some of them may have pictures and photos, which would make the history even more interesting.

You can share the information you gather by printing it up and distributing it, making it available through the school or public library, recording it on video or audio cassette, or creating a display to set up in a public place. Be sure to include credits: "This history project was researched and produced by the Poplar Road service group." This ensures that you get the credit you deserve and lets people know who they can contact for more information.

Time Capsule

A time capsule is a sealed container that holds documents and items of historical interest to future citizens. You can collect and create items of possible historical interest, label them, include notes and explanations, seal them in a container, and set the capsule in a place for future historians. Include ordinary, everyday objects: toys, games, books, magazines, notebooks, tools, and newspaper articles on current events. Popular culture is always important—music, fashion, fads, and so on. You can write a "letter to the future" from your entire group, or individual letters describing your life, school, home, town, and self. You can also include some of the materials from an oral-history project.

Work with the school or other local authorities to place the time capsule in a secure place and leave a message to the future so it will be known when to open it. Include a notice letting people know who did the project, and be sure to publicize it.

Tutoring

What is your best academic subject? Did one subject give you a hard time until you finally managed to master it? You can help other students or members of your community by tutoring a certain number of hours per week in a particular subject. With the school administration and faculty, arrange a time and place for the tutoring, and for supplies and materials, and let people know through flyers,

PA announcements, and word-of-mouth. Or if there is a tutoring program in your school or community (often through the public library), contact them and see how you can help. The program may need materials as well as tutors. If there isn't a tutoring program, you may want to help get one going. For information and assistance, contact Quest International, Literacy Volunteers of America (they deal mostly with adults but maybe able to provide useful information), and your local public library.

You can also give instruction in non-academic subjects—bicycle maintenance and repair, sports and games, sewing, crafts, pet care, gardening, dance, music, art, and much more. Set aside a certain time and place each week (or some other regular interval) for people to come to you, or you can go to them. Use flyers, word-of-mouth, bulletins boards, and other means to let people know about your service. This project can be done through schools, churches, synagogues, community centers, libraries, or even in private homes (check with a trustworthy adult before going to anyone's home or inviting anyone into your home).

Before you advertise your services, be sure you have everything on hand—tools, books, equipment, or whatever it is you need for teaching.

Literacy and English as a Second Language (ESL) Instruction

Thousands of people living in the United States are functionally illiterate: Either they can't read and write at all or they read so poorly that their comprehension of what they read is negligible. Comparable to this is the plight of people living in the U.S. for whom English is a second language. Both predicaments can effectively cripple a person's social, professional, and personal progress, and people in either of these categories can use your help.

Your community may offer literacy programs through the public library or adult-education branch of the school district. Look up the programs in the phone book and contact them to see how you can help, either by actual tutoring or in some other way, such as donating materials, administrative work, and so forth. Literacy tutoring is among the most rewarding services you can perform—but it requires a serious commitment. First, there is usually a training period, which varies from program to program but will probably involve at least one day. Once you're trained, most programs require that you agree to serve for several weeks or months, with a minimum commitment of a few hours (usually at least two) per week.

If your community doesn't offer a literacy program, you can start one. Although Literacy Volunteers of America (see Chapter 9) only accepts adult volunteers, they can send you detailed instructions on how to do this, as well as help in getting funding.

Loan Closets

Loan closets contain items that students or community members may need temporarily. Items are signed out to borrowers, as in a library, for use in school, at home, at a community center, church, and so forth. For example, a school home-economics loan closet would contain cooking utensils; an art loan closet would contain art supplies; and so on. You can also create a recreational loan closet or a general-supplies closet (rulers, pens, staplers, and so forth). A community loan closet could offer yard and household tools—hedge clippers, shovels, hammers, wrenches, and so forth—or implements for cooking, repairs and gardening.

To start your loan closet you'll need to find a secure storage location—make sure you have this place set up before you collect anything. Then you'll need to collect (or buy or solicit) appropriate items, and make an index-card file of what you have. For checking things in and out, keep cards in two separate boxes: an IN box and an OUT box. Whenever someone checks something out, write their name, phone number, and any other useful information (grade, address, and so forth) on the card for that item. Before the borrower takes the item, record the condition it's in—write down specifics of any dents and damage. Make sure the borrower knows when the item is due back (a week, two days, whatever has been decided before-hand). You may have to call and remind people of late items, and you may never get some items back, but there are ways of keeping losses to a minimum. Talk to a librarian for help setting up and running your system.

Signs and Buddies for Newcomers

Did you ever get lost on your first day at a new school? Forget your locker number or combination? Miss lunch because you couldn't find the cafeteria? Arrive late because you got lost? Miss your bus? Something like this has happened to all of us. You can help new students avoid getting lost by putting up signs during the first few weeks of school to indicate directions to specific rooms (cafeteria, gym, bathrooms, office), and making sure all rooms have a clearly visible name or number. Recruit volunteers to serve as "buddies" to new students (or residents) to help show them around in the first few weeks.

This idea can also be adapted for new neighbors: Introduce yourself, help your new neighbor find where things are (grocery store, bus stop, library), and generally help him or her feel a little less lost.

A variation on this project is to print a booklet for newcomers that helps them get to know the school or neighborhood. Include the kind of "unofficial" information that helps make people feel at home, like what the best (and worst) cafeteria food is, where the good restaurants are, where people hang out, what activities are available, which places are fun and safe and which should be avoided, and other tidbits that you've learned through experience.

Honor Cooks, Custodians, Mail Carriers, and Trash Collectors

Without janitors or cooks, your school would be dirty, smelly, and full of hungry, cranky people—a frightening prospect indeed. The cafeteria and janitorial staff provide services so basic that we often take them for granted. They receive little or no recognition for their efforts. You can recognize their contributions in various ways:

❑ Create a badge or ribbon especially for them and present it to them at an assembly or other public gathering.
❑ Give them a certificate of appreciation or small gift.

❏ Make a creative "corsage" (see Chapter 3 for more information).
❏ Thank them over the PA system and in the school bulletin or newspaper.

This project can also work for community workers, such as garbage collectors, gardeners, maintenance workers, mail carriers, and so forth. Think what your community would be like without them! Let them know you realize how important their work is and that you appreciate it.

Cards, Courtesy, and Sympathy

When a student, staff member, or someone in your community is in the hospital, homebound for an extended period of time because of illness, or suffering from some other misfortune, such as the death of a loved one, send him or her a card, and if possible, visit. In the event of the death of a student or staff member, send flowers and/or visit the family. Buy or make a card, pass it around so everyone can sign it, and send it along with flowers. You can buy flowers and deliver them yourself, or you can order them at a florist's shop and have them deliver the flowers. The shop will usually also deliver your card, if you have one, along with the flowers.

Murals and Artwork

The difference between a blank stretch of dreary wall and a colorful stretch of original artwork is like a bare patch of dirt compared to a flower garden. Artwork is a great way to brighten up an environment. If you know of a site in your school or community that could use some brightening, consider creating a mural or some form of artwork to help beautify your surroundings.

While it is possible to do this entirely on your own, it is more likely to be a collaborative effort, involving teachers, parents, community volunteers, local artists, and others. This is the kind of project that benefits enormously from outside help.

Time and Money.   Depending on complexity of design, hours worked per day, size, and other factors, it can take anywhere from a single day to a month to actually paint your mural—not including the time needed for designing, soliciting help, getting permits, and so forth. The cost also varies according to these factors, ranging between $200 and $1,000, and depending on how much of the materials and skills you can get donated (see Chapter 8). So be prepared to do some fund-raising and soliciting.

Sites and Permission.   Consider the following when locating a space:

- ❏ Visibility: Can it be seen?
- ❏ Accessibility: Can you get to it to work on it?
- ❏ Safety: Can you work on your mural safely? Will your work create a disturbance or hazard for others?

Once you've located a likely site or two (it doesn't hurt to have an alternative in case your first choice doesn't work out), get permission from whomever is in charge of that site. If it's on school property, talk to the principal or school-district authorities. If it's on private property, such as an office or apartment building, speak to the owner or manager. If it's on public property, such as a freeway overpass or municipal building, contact the city authorities—try the department of public works or the city manager's office. Always get written permission—a document, signed letter, or permit; something official you can show people in case there are any questions about your right to conduct your project.

Getting permission will probably involve submitting your designs and plans for approval. The people in charge will want to make sure the design is appropriate and that you can complete the project in a timely and organized manner. So before asking for permission, have a design and general plan.

Create a Design.   You can create a design yourself or involve local artists and/or art students. Working with professional artists will help ensure the quality of your project, but be prepared to pay something—after all, this is how they make their living. Some artists might be willing to negotiate. Art students, for example, might be willing to work for free for the exposure the project would give their work. To contact them, post flyers at art schools, galleries, cafes, and other places where artists and art students congregate. The content of your mural can be an abstract design, a tribute to some hero or ideal, a positive expression of an important issue, a celebration or memorial of an important event, or just plain decorative. Keep it accessible, positive, and broad-minded. Make sure the design is aesthetically pleasing. For ideas and assistance, see *Wallworks: Creating Unique Environments with Surface Design and Decoration*, by Akiko Busch (See Chapter 9), and check your public library for more help and ideas.

When creating a design, there are several factors to keep in mind:

❏ If you're executing the mural yourself, keep it simple. In the city where I live, there are several murals by junior high-school students that are quite simple but very striking and attractive. One is a design of brightly colored stars stencilled onto a multicolored background of large stripes. Another is handprints on a bright background. Use your imagination.

❏ Make sure your theme is universal enough to stand up to the test of time. For example, a mural honoring a person should make sure that people in 20 years will still know who she or he is and that what the person stood for was honorable.

❏ Make sure your design doesn't clash with its surroundings. See the box below on Public Art Do's and Don'ts for additional tips.

Locate Paint, Materials, and Expertise.   Paint is the most important factor determining your mural's durability, so don't skimp on it. You need plenty of high-quality, water-based (for the environment) acrylic paint. Measure out how many square feet you need of each color, and ask a salesperson at a paint store to help you estimate how much you'll need.

You'll also need dropcloths to protect surrounding sidewalks and fences, paintbrushes and rollers, and protective caps and clothing for the painters. Think of this as an opportunity to get the community

Public Art Do's and Don'ts

❑ **Do** observe the boundaries of good taste and dignity. While taste is subject to local community standards, avoid vulgarity of any kind. Explicit or indirect sexual content, obscenities, and violence of any kind are unacceptable. It's a work of art, not a dirty joke or splatter film.

❑ **Do** respect others' opinions, sensibilities, and heritage. If you live near a large Native-American population, for example, a mural glorifying Christopher Columbus might not be a welcome addition to the neighborhood. A conservative senior home might not be the best place for that radical hip-hop design you've created. You get the idea.

❑ **DON'T** disrespect any person or group in any way, directly or indirectly. Your message must be entirely free of racism, sexism, prejudice, and stereotypes.

❑ **DON'T** glorify someone or some group at the expense of another: "Berkeley beats Stanford!" may be an appropriate slogan for a pep rally, but hardly for a lasting monument.

❑ **Do** comply with these tenets or risk having your mural denied, "tagged" (marred by graffiti), or destroyed. Not long ago at a prominent university, students submitted a design for a mural honoring a national hero, which was approved. But when they painted the actual mural, they added a border incorporating racist symbols that had not been in the submitted plans and which greatly offended many people. After a great deal of name-calling, finger-pointing, and general belligerence, the mural was painted over. The incident caused considerable bad feeling and wasted a lot of hard work.

involved—especially hardware stores, who may help you by donating supplies. See Chapter 8 for tips on enlisting help from businesses.

Give Credit to All. When the mural is completed, include information about who did the mural and who helped. In the lower right-hand corner (or somewhere else that's visible but doesn't interfere with the design), write something like: "Mural created by the Diamond Heights Service Club and artists Sylvia Chang and Barry Patel. Materials and funding graciously donated by Silver's Hardware Store, the City of Riverdale, Gina's Pizza, and the PTA." Be sure to remember everyone who helped.

Alternatives to Murals. If a mural isn't feasible, you can still beautify your school or street with other kinds of art displays (permanent or temporary), such as paintings, sculptures, and all kinds of crafts, set up at schools, government buildings, malls, and so forth. Consult the proper authorities to find out what kind of art would be feasible and appropriate.

Counseling, Mediation, and Conflict Resolution

Do the same kinds of conflicts seem to flare up again and again in your school or community? Do you see a lot of people who don't seem to be able to resolve their problems and conflicts peacefully? Do you know of kids who go for days without a friendly word from anyone, at home or at school? Anger, problems, and conflict are an inevitable part of life. It's impossible to avoid them, but we can all learn to manage them successfully and productively, and help others do the same. You may be able to help through peer counseling, peer mediation, or conflict-resolution programs.

Peer counseling normally consists of one-on-one sessions in which trained counselors lend a friendly, sympathetic ear to a fellow student or teen. It's mostly just listening and asking helpful questions. It's not a substitute for professional therapy, but it can be enormously helpful to someone who needs to talk.

Peer mediation usually involves two mediators who help their peers resolve some kind of conflict in a safe, productive way. It could be a boyfriend–girlfriend issue, academic competition, two guys after the same girl, friends hitting a rough patch in their relationship, or something similar. The mediators guide the people having the problem toward a resolution, which often consists of a written agreement that all parties sign, indicating expectations, behavior, limitations, and other agreed-upon measures.

Conflict resolution is usually a series of 10 to 25 sessions that lead young people through a process of identifying and coping with anger points. It emphasizes self-control and stress management so participants learn to manage their emotions and resolve problems without violence.

This kind of project involves serious commitment—some programs require a three-year plan. You would need to work with teachers, counselors, parents, or other adults, since this involves legal issues, privacy, record-keeping, and other matters that require careful planning, monitoring, and accountability. Counseling or mediation also involves training, often quite intensive, and a minimum time commitment of at least a couple of hours per week. It isn't easy to keep the peace! However, it is among the most rewarding projects you can undertake, one that not only helps you give a lasting gift to your community, but also benefits you directly in ways that will endure for the rest of your life.

Several organizations provide training in peer counseling, mediation, and conflict resolution, as well as referrals to existing programs nationwide. The National Youth Leadership Council is a good source of information and referrals. Other organizations to contact for help and information are Quest International, the National Association for Mediation in Education (NAME), the Character Education Partnership, and the Josephson Institute of Ethics. See the resource section (Chapter 9) for these and other listings. In addition, talk to your school counselor, and check his or her professional journals and periodicals for information about programs and resources. There are also many different kinds of community-based counseling and mediation activities worth investigating. Check your local phone book for counselors and therapists or lawyers and union leaders.

Start a Support Group

Life is full of problems, and we all need a little support now and then to help us cope and let us know we're not alone. Support groups are a simple but effective way of accomplishing this. A support group is simply a group of people who gather regularly to share their experiences and feelings about a certain issue in their lives. It can be as simple as a bunch of people sitting in someone's living room talking, or a structured session led by a moderator or facilitator, or a more formal seminar led by professionals. The topic can be anything you feel is important. What kinds of concerns are you and your friends grappling with? It could be depression, problems with parents, academic performance, drugs and alcohol, gangs, violence, sexual issues, parenthood, unemployment, or anything affecting you, your friends, and your family. Getting together once a week or so just to talk may not seem like much, but you may be surprised at how helpful it can be to alleviate feelings of anxiety, loneliness, and stress. It's also an excellent way to exchange practical ideas and information.

All you really need is a place to meet, which can be someone's kitchen, a classroom, a table in the cafeteria, or a patch of lawn (in nice weather). Many companies, schools, hospitals, and non-profit organizations have conference rooms or classrooms available for use. Then you need to set a regular schedule—and stick to it. One of the prime directives of a support group is consistency; it should always be there when it's supposed to be.

Once you have a topic, place, and schedule, get the word out. Flyers and word-of-mouth are probably your best bets, and you may also want to post notices on bulletin boards (on walls *and* computers). For assistance and information, contact the American Self-Help Clearinghouse (see resource listings in Chapter 9).

Other School and Community Activities

❏ Plant trees or gardens (see Chapter 6 for details).
❏ Clean chalkboards and walls.
❏ Encourage your school or housing sector or building to "adopt" a senior home, hospital, homeless shelter, food bank, or other organization.
❏ Contribute to (or create) the school or neighborhood newspaper.
❏ Sponsor a safety-awareness campaign: Contact the local Red Cross, fire department, hospitals, or police about free or low-cost courses in CPR (cardiopulmonary resuscitation), fire safety, crime prevention, and general health and safety awareness.

Things You Should Know About Tutoring, Counseling, and Mediation Programs

❑ One of the first steps in establishing such a program is a needs assessment: Do some research to pinpoint what kinds of services are needed and what may already exist in your community to address those needs. Don't reinvent the wheel.

❑ It's often useful to work with an established club or organization in the school or community (Key Club, Scouts, and so forth) that offers an existing structure in which to operate; you can also work with community organizations such as Lions' Clubs, which may be able to provide valuable skills, resources, funding, and services. Take advantage of what your community has to offer.

❑ You stack the deck for success when you make it a true community initiative and include as many segments of the community as possible.

❑ It's a long-term commitment, since it involves strategic planning to ensure effectiveness and promote consistency and follow-up—two of the keys to a successful program of this kind.

❑ Everyone in the school or community benefits, but especially those who go through the training, for they develop far-reaching skills that stay with them the rest of their lives.

❑ Many young people who become involved in these programs discover vital interests and talents of their own, and some go on to pursue these activities on a professional basis. This could be the start of a career.

❑ Build for the future—it's your legacy.

—From Quest International

❑ Set up a "sister school" or city or neighborhood program with a school or city or neighborhood in another district, state, or country. Plan activities with the common goal of getting to know students and teachers from another area.

❑ Provide a juice-and-cookies break for students and teachers during standardized test days.

6

The

Environment

According to Native American tradition, no important decision is made until the following question is asked: "How will this decision affect the seventh generation?" Those making the decision try to determine what impact any course of action will have on their own great-great-great-great-great grandchildren. All societies would do well to emulate this recognition of responsibility to the future and of the consequences of one's actions and decisions. In this spirit, think of projects to improve the environment, which benefit not only those of us alive today, but also those not yet born. They may never be able to thank you, but future generations will owe you a debt of gratitude.

Many environmental projects can benefit greatly from collaboration with local environmental organizations. There may be chapters of national organizations, such as the Sierra Club or Audubon Society, in your area, and many towns have their own local environmental groups. These groups are likely to know about such things as local recycling capabilities, businesses and organizations sympathetic to environmental concerns, sources of funds and materials, local projects and activities, and what kinds of services are needed and feasible.

Recycle

Recycling efforts can be as modest as a small project done by you and your friends, such as recycling aluminum, plastic, and glass at home or recycling cans from a party or event, or it can involve the entire school or city. First of all, be sure you're doing what you can by recycling at home before you go out to exhort the public: Practice what you preach. Your family may readily cooperate, but even if there is some resistance, you can still do your part by recycling what *you* use.

Once things are humming on the home front, the next step is to initiate, expand, or somehow participate in recycling activities in your school, in which case you'll need to work with other students, teachers, and administrators. Collect and distribute information on which materials can be recycled and what would be the best way to recycle. Contact local recycling authorities to get information and their support and assistance; they probably know how to conduct campaigns of this kind and may have ready-made materials and activities.

One of the first things you need to do to start a recycling program in your community or school is to get a clear picture of local recycling capabilities. Check the White Pages under the city government listings for your local department of solid waste, or other listings for agencies that handle trash pickup. Also check the Yellow Pages under "Recycling" or "Waste Management." See what recycling centers will accept, and how much they pay (if anything). Ask about collection services. Some cities have curbside collection; others require taking items to the nearest recycling centers.

Get this information to key people in your school—student government, administration, influential teachers, PTA officers—and make it clear that you are willing to do whatever work needs to be done.

Establish a Recycling Center

If there are no recycling facilities in your community, you may want to mobilize the community to establish one. This endeavor requires a lot of community involvement and cooperation. Dozens of organizations around the country are committed to helping communities start or expand their recycling efforts and capabilities (see the resource listings in Chapter 9). Because local circumstances are so different, we cannot go into detail on how to establish a center here. It will undoubtedly take a significant amount of work and a fairly long-term commitment—these things don't happen overnight. In the long run, your efforts are likely to be received very positively, as most people now recognize the need for and advantages of recycling. Any time and energy you invest in a project of this type would be well worth it, since you will help your entire community for generations to come.

The Environmental Defense Fund (EDF) has access to (or information about) many excellent resources for helping communities develop recycling programs without reinventing the wheel. For example, the "peer match" program brings together local groups who want to recycle with experts familiar with the particular problems of local and state recycling efforts. For further information, contact the EDF, listed in Chapter 9, or your state waste-management or natural-resources bureau.

Conduct a Recycling Drive

Conduct this project in your school or neighborhood, on a scale as small as your block or as large as the whole town. Collect newspaper, aluminum cans, foil, tin cans, clear and colored glass, and recyclable plastic, or one or more of these items. (See Chapter 8 for collection-drive instructions.) When the items to be recycled have been collected, they need to be sorted according to the guidelines of your local recycling center. For example, some recycling centers can't recycle glossy or other chemically treated paper, so the glossy sections in newspapers may have to be discarded. Check with your local recycling center for specific guidelines.

This project may also help raise funds for some other project, since many recyclable items are redeemable for cash in some states. Check with local recyclers to find out if they pay and how much (rates vary from week to week).

Recycling Bins for Your School or Neighborhood

Talk to your school administrator, student council, housing-authority representative, building supervisor, or neighborhood alliance about placing bins in selected sites for recycling paper, glass, plastic, and aluminum. This project could work in an apartment building or compound, school, public-housing development, senior home, neighborhood, office, or anywhere that people live, work, play, or spend free time.

This project needs to be coordinated with local recycling facilities. If they have pickup service, arrange times, dates, and types of containers and items they prefer. If they don't, you'll need volunteers with vans or pickup trucks to take the items to the recycling facility regularly (for example, once a week, twice a month).

If the recycling center doesn't provide containers, contact local building-supply, hardware, and paint stores to obtain barrels and other large containers. Label the containers clearly with signs indicating what they are for: RECYCLE YOUR SODA CANS HERE. Consult with the managers of the places where you plan to put the containers to decide on placement. For example, in the school cafeteria near the trash cans, you can set up two barrels—one for glass, and one for aluminum (soft-drink cans and foil). You can also set out barrels for recycling paper in classrooms and hallways. In a housing development, place clearly marked barrels near the garbage facilities.

Publicize your recycling canisters with flyers, posters, announcements, and perhaps some kind of kick-off ceremony. Make sure everyone knows about the recycling containers and how to use them. Post clear instructions about what can and can't be recycled and what goes where. For the first few days, place volunteers by the barrels to remind people what to recycle.

Another way to encourage people to start recycling is to offer rewards. For example, you can give out a small prize or treat to those who put their cans, bottles, papers, and so forth in the recycling bins (see Chapter 8 on how to get a local business to contribute the prizes or gifts). Or give out raffle tickets as the reward, and get, say, a record, toy, or clothing store to donate a gift certificate as the raffle prize.

Even with instructions, people will make mistakes, so the contents of the barrels may need to be sorted before they can be recycled.

Compost

Recycling is not just about bottles, cans, and paper. Another 20 percent of household garbage can also be recycled by composting. Compost is basically organic garbage—coffee grounds, teabags, fruit and vegetable peels, egg shells, leaves, weeds, and other organic wastes—and it is very good for the soil. Nature composts itself automatically: Leaves fall, rot, and return to the soil to feed the tree

How to Make Fireplace Logs from Newspaper

Use old paper to make excellent fireplace logs without burning any trees. You can use the logs at home, donate them to institutions and needy homes that have fireplaces, or sell them to raise money.

You'll need:
- ❏ Containers large enough to hold several soaking newspaper logs (buckets, trashcans, etc.)
- ❏ Stacks of old newspapers (continuous-fold computer paper can be used as well)
- ❏ Twine or string (each piece should be at least a 1½ feet long)
- ❏ Sturdy sticks or dowels about two feet long
- ❏ Scissors
- ❏ Water.

Instructions:
1. Take a stack of about eight pages of newspaper and lay them out flat. Lay the stick on top of the paper.
2. Roll the newspaper around the stick (like a roll of paper towels) until about eight inches of paper are left. Add another stack of eight

from which they fell. The only organic waste that's not good for compost is meat of any kind.

Most local environmental organizations will be able to connect you with some person or group that can teach you how to compost. It's pretty simple, but there are a few tricks you need to know. For more information, see the environmental resource listings in Chapter 9. Your own town or state probably has some information on composting, so check your phone book or government directory.

Here are some things you can do with your compost:

- ❏ Give it to local farmers and growers to use as fertilizer.
- ❏ Use it in gardens and lawns.
- ❏ Give it to the school (or other facility) gardener to use as fertilizer.

newspaper pages so that it overlaps with the paper sticking out from the roll. Continue rolling and adding paper until you have a good-sized log. The stick should protrude at each end.

3. Tie the roll of paper with the twine or string so it doesn't unroll; each roll should be tied twice, about three inches from each end.

4. Soak the tied rolls (with sticks still in them) overnight in water.

5. The next day, take the soaked logs out of the water. Bang and roll them on the ground to pack the paper tightly and get rid of excess water.

6. Remove the stick and dry the logs *thoroughly*, on a rack, in direct sunlight if possible. (This may take a day or two.)

❏ You can get rid of the musty smell by adding a few drops of flower-essence oil to the water or by tucking in bits of incense among the paper. Don't use too much scent, and don't use anything that people might be allergic to or that might produce toxic fumes.

❏ Use the water you soaked the logs in to water plants, trees, or gardens.

❏ Contact your local parks and recreation or city maintenance departments to find out if they can use compost in municipal gardens and parks.

Other Environmental Projects

While recycling is probably the most common type of environmental activity, there are many other areas of concern where your help is needed—and effective. Our air, water, soil, and surroundings are all part of the environment, and are all interconnected. Anything you can do to help, say, the air, often has beneficial effects in other areas, such as the water and soil.

Smog-free Days

Work with your school administration, neighbors, and/or community leaders to designate a particular day as a "Smog-Free Day," on which no one can use a car except for emergencies and car-pooling. Use publicity and incentives to encourage people to use public transportation, bicycles, walking, and other alternatives to driving. This type of activity works best in a small town, public-housing site, school, or other unified environment, but it can be modified or expanded for city use. Consult with the mayor, environmental organizations, the school district, the parks and recreation department, or civic, youth, and church organizations to promote your Smog-Free campaign.

With the help of these organizations, get the local media to help (see publicity tips in Chapter 8), and develop informational materials (a fact sheet, handout, or flyer) to let people know about alternatives to automobiles. List streets with bike paths, bus routes, subways, car-pool stations, and ferries, along with the advantages of each. Public-works, police, parks and recreation, and transit departments can help you put together information; much of it may already be collected somewhere. Raise awareness by including information about the environmental damage cars cause and how much it helps to minimize driving. Get this data out to your target audience in a timely and persuasive manner.

You may also want to offer incentives for using alternative transportation. Perhaps you could work with local restaurants and retailers to offer coupons, discounts, or freebies to all those who don't drive on the designated day (see Chapter 8 for tips). Or you can recruit a group of volunteers willing to work a few hours for free at such tasks as gardening, washing cars, babysitting, and anything else you feel willing and able to do: You can organize a group to give out vouchers good for, say, an hour of free work to each non-driver.

Set an Example

If you're going to help your community protect the environment, your group must set an example by:

❏ Using recyclables—paper plates and cups instead of Styrofoam or plastic, for example—and setting out bins for cans and bottles at gatherings
❏ Using recycled paper whenever possible
❏ Using both sides of paper
❏ Bringing lunches in reusable (cloth) bags or lunch boxes
❏ Avoiding food and other products with a lot of packaging, especially if it's plastic, and using reusable containers for food storage
❏ Helping your families to recycle; using cloth shopping bags, and so forth.

Monitor Acid Rain

Because our air is so polluted, the rain that falls is also polluted. It's called "acid rain," and is harmful to trees, plants, wildlife, and people. You can measure how "acid" the rain in your area is and let people know about it. For information about acid rain and how to create a test kit to monitor it in your region, contact Citizen's Acid Rain Monitoring Network at the National Audubon Society (see the animal and wildlife resource section in Chapter 9 for the address).

Plant Trees

Trees help decrease the build-up of carbon dioxide in the air and give us clean oxygen to breathe, which means less smog and acid rain. They also beautify our surroundings and provide us with fruit, nuts, and shade. And watching a tree appear and grow with the help of your efforts really gives you a sense of long-term accomplishment. It's a very "seventh generation" thing to do.

There are many organizations that provide materials and instructions for planting trees. Many highway, transportation, forestry, and parks and recreation departments have tree-planting programs. Some other organizations and programs that encourage tree-planting are the International Center for Development Policy's New Forests Project, National Arbor Day Foundation, Global Re-Leaf, and more—see Chapter 9. These organizations can tell you how

How to Make Paper

You'll need:

- ❑ 2½ single pages from a newspaper
- ❑ A whole section of a newspaper
- ❑ A blender
- ❑ Water (about a gallon)
- ❑ A big square pan that's at least three inches deep
- ❑ A piece of window screen that fits inside the pan
- ❑ A measuring cup
- ❑ A flat piece of wood the size of a double newspaper page.

Instructions:

1. Tear the 2½ pages of newspaper into tiny pieces.
2. Drop the pieces into the blender.
3. Pour five cups of water into the blender.
4. Turn on the blender (cover it first) until the paper becomes pulp.
5. Pour about one inch of water into the pan.
6. Put the screen into the pan so that the screen is under water.
7. Pour one cup of paper pulp from the blender over the screen in the pan.
8. Spread the pulp around with your fingers until it's evenly spread—not too thin, or your paper will be too flimsy, and not too thick, or your paper will be too bulky, like lumpy cardboard.

to go about choosing a site, clearing plans with the proper authorities, acquiring seeds or saplings, and caring for your trees.

Plant a Garden

A garden beautifies your school or neighborhood and provides flowers as gifts for the sick and fruits and vegetables to feed the hungry.

You'll need permission to use a bit of open ground that receives some sunlight, some seeds and/or starter plants, basic gardening tools (a spade and shears, or even just a big sturdy spoon and scissors),

9. Open the newspaper section to the middle.
10. Lift the screen (keep it flat) with the paper pulp on it and let the water drain back into the pan.
11. Place the screen with the pulp on one side of the newspaper section.
12. Close the newspaper with the screen and pulp inside it.
13. *Very carefully* flip the newspaper section over so that the screen is on top of the pulp.
14. Place the board on top of the newspaper, and press down to squeeze the excess water out of the pulp.
15. Open the newspaper and remove the screen; leave the pulp.
16. Leave the newspaper open (out of the wind, near a sunny window if possible), and let the pulp dry for at least 24 hours.
17. When the pulp is *completely* dry, carefully peel it off the newspaper.
18. You can jazz up this recipe by adding a few drops of food coloring to the paper and water in the blender. If you add the food coloring before blending, the color will be even. If you mix the coloring in after blending the paper and water, the color will come out in spots and swirls. You can also mix in tiny shreds of colored yarn, cloth, or thread to the paper pulp before you pour it out of the blender.

You can also purchase paper-making kits at art and craft stores.

access to water, and plant food or fertilizer (see the section on compost, above).

There are many useful instructional materials about gardening for young people. My particular favorite is *Kids Gardening: A Kid's Guide to Messing Around in the Dirt*, by Kim and Kevin Rafferty, which was written for younger children, but is very clear and complete. It has amusing illustrations and detailed but easy instructions for indoor and outdoor gardening. It comes with packets of flower and vegetable seeds and is an excellent activity guide for all ages. See the publications section in the environmental resource listings in Chapter 9 for details and more books and manuals.

More Recycling and Environmental Activities

❏ Pick up litter from a park, beach, and the like, and sort and recycle it.
❏ Collect and repair old lawn tools and furniture.
❏ Distribute recycling information in your school and/or community; conduct a recycling-awareness campaign.
❏ Plan a tour of a recycling, waste-disposal, or water-purification center.
❏ Conduct a letter-writing campaign to town officials to encourage recycling services (addresses can be obtained at the public library).
❏ Write letters to manufacturers of overpackaged products expressing your concern and suggesting alternative packaging ideas; let them know you buy "green." Addresses of manufacturers are usually on the packages.
❏ Conduct a letter-writing campaign to local, national, or world leaders letting them know how you feel about saving the earth. You can obtain addresses of U.S. leaders (senators, judges, the president) at your public library. For leaders of other countries, try the library or write to the countries' representatives at the United Nations (see Chapter 9).
❏ Make and sell or give away recycling bins for home and office use.
❏ Put up recycling and environmental window displays or posters in local businesses, malls, parks, shopping centers, and other appropriate places.
❏ Make and use cloth shopping bags to carry groceries and other purchases, and sell or give them away at shopping centers. You can do the same thing with reusable lunch bags.
❏ Develop a display for fairs and conferences. Themes might include: "green" shopping, composting, renewable vs. nonrenewable resources, and recycling in your community.
❏ Develop a presentation on environmental activities to present to other youth groups, neighborhood coalitions, school and city officials, civic groups and clubs, parent groups, and many other organizations.

Adoption Programs

A wide variety of adoption programs are sponsored by local, state, and national organizations and government agencies: adopt-a-high-

- Give an annual award for good environmental practices.
- Develop and distribute a list of environmentally safe school, office, and/or household materials and supplies—and use them.
- Make use of foreign-exchange programs to learn about resource use and environmental policies in other countries.
- Fill washed, empty egg shells with soil and plant seeds. As plants begin to grow, they can be planted, shell and all. The shell will decompose and nourish the soil.
- Plan and conduct a periodic (for example, twice a year) garage sale to encourage reusing household items.
- Make quilted or insulated shades for windows to help conserve energy and lower heating bills, especially for elderly and needy people.
- Learn about a rain-forest tribe to acquire a greater appreciation for the endangered rain forests; contact Cultural Survival, listed in Chapter 9.
- Find out which companies have good environmental practices, such as using recycled packaging, protecting the rain forest, preventing pollution, and so forth, and let people know about them so they (and you) can use these companies' products instead of buying things from companies that damage the environment. You can get this information from the public library or some of the organizations listed in Chapter 9.
- Make a list of resolutions for the environment, describing what you want for the environment and what you can do to help achieve these aims; for example, "more trees—plant trees," or "cleaner air—walk, bike, or use public transportation instead of driving."

Letters can also be e-mailed or posted on computer bulletin boards.

way, adopt-a-beach, adopt-a-park, etc. Your group can sign on to care for a designated area and agree to keep it clean, beautify it, tend plants, and so forth. Adoption periods vary, from monthly to yearly.

Most of these programs require a minimum commitment, such as cleaning up a certain number of times per year. Most agencies with programs of this sort will provide varying degrees of assistance and resources: information, manuals, trashbags, special events, instruction, and so forth. Some operate with related organizations, such as recycling centers for disposing of trash in an environmentally sound manner.

Adopt-a-Highway.   Many departments of transportation have an "Adopt-a-Highway" program, or some variation on it, in which a specific group of people agrees to take care of a specific stretch of road. They keep it free of trash, tend the greenery, and generally beautify their territory with flowers, plants, and trees. Trash is often sorted, either later or as it is collected, for recycling (if it isn't, you may want to suggest it anyway). Some transportation departments place a sign on your territory displaying the name of your group.

Adopt-a-Beach.   Check with the department of parks and recreation, coastal commission, and other agencies involved with beaches, lakes, and rivers to ask about this kind of project and what their requirements are. In addition to trash recycling, many beach cleanup programs include wildlife assistance to help creatures that get hurt or trapped in litter or oil spills.

Adopt-a-Tree.   While your town or neighborhood may have a program for "adopting" a tree, no program is necessary. Select a tree that seems as if it could use a bit of care, and take care of it. Ask local nurseries for help.

Adopt-a-Piece-of-Earth.   Find a plot of ground that could use some attention, and take care of it—keep it clean, weed it, water it, plant some flowers, put up a bird-feeder and/or birdbath. You can turn an eyesore into a haven of beauty with a bit of regular work.

See Chapter 7 on animals and wildlife for more adoption programs.

7

Animal Care
and Wildlife

As our knowledge of the earth and the interrelationships of ecological systems grows, we have become more and more aware of the vital role animals play in the delicate balance that sustains all life. Animals are a very important part of the environment—and our lives. Without them the balance of nature would be upset, and we would be overrun with bugs, rats, or garbage. Besides being necessary to the continuing survival of the earth and our own species, animals have a right to exist, just as we do.

Help for Domestic Animals

If you have a pet, you probably take good care of it and keep it safe and healthy. Unfortunately, not everyone does. There are many neglected and abused cats and dogs and other pets who end up hungry or sick or dead on the streets. Fortunately, you can do something to help them.

Supplies for the Animal Shelter

Contact your local animal shelter, ASPCA, or Humane Society to find out what they need and whom to contact about arranging such a project. Some animal shelters are under the authority of the city or town in which they're located. Contact the city manager's office to find out the exact department and/or individual who can approve a gift to the animal shelter, since many can't accept gifts without authorization.

Pet food is often a welcome item. Most shelters don't use flea collars or other accessories treated with chemicals to which some animals might be allergic. But dog biscuits and chew toys may be used, as well as blankets and bedding. You can conduct a collection drive for these, donate what you can, or ask local markets to help out. You will learn something if you personally deliver the items too, and see firsthand what happens to animals when people don't take good care of them.

Get Animals Placed in Homes

Many animal shelters conduct annual or semiannual pet placement drives, usually in the spring, when there are lots of baby animals and the shelters are overcrowded. They often set up a display with cages full of kittens and puppies at shopping centers and busy street corners. You can help staff the displays and persuade people to take home a kitten or puppy. Who can resist the request of a winsome youngster (that's you) holding a kitten or puppy? Contact the manager of the animal shelter to ask if they do such placement drives, and suggest they do so if they don't and offer to volunteer. Find out how you can help. Having a placement station in front of your school, especially at the end of the day when parents arrive, can be quite useful. But don't give pets to children without their parents' permission, since these pets often end up right back in the pound.

Other Ways to Help Animal Shelters

You can offer shelters a helping hand by cleaning out cages and facilities, or repairing and painting them.

You can also volunteer to collect new cages, equipment, and so forth. Call the local animal shelter for details and ideas.

Help for Wildlife

Animals have suffered greatly at the hands of humans as we have taken over so much of the earth's surface, damaged the land and water, and hunted animals to the brink of extinction. There are many ways you can help wild animals without interfering with their natural patterns and habitats. In addition to the projects listed here, try writing to some of the organizations listed in the resource section in Chapter 9 to discover other ways in which you can help.

How to Build a Birdhouse

You'll need:
- ❏ An empty half-gallon cardboard milk carton
- ❏ A pair of scissors
- ❏ About two feet of wire, light enough to bend, strong enough to hold the weight of the birdhouse, and a little thinner than clothes-hanger wire
- ❏ Two medium-size nails and a hammer
- ❏ A clump of dried grass
- ❏ Some waterproof packing tape.

Instructions:
1. Completely open up the top of the milk carton (carefully—don't rip it all up) and clean it out well.
2. Cut a hole about the size of a doorknob in one side of the carton, a couple of inches below where the top folds. This will be the bird's "door," so make sure the edges are smooth, with no jagged edges on which the bird can get hurt or stuck.
3. On the opposite side of the carton, make two puncture holes with a nail. The top hole should be about one-third of the way down from

The Zoo

In addition to being a lot of fun to visit, zoos help protect animals and make sure certain species survive. If it weren't for zoos, for instance, the panda might not be around any more. Zoos can always use some help. Call the volunteer-services department at the local zoo to see what kinds of projects might be available for you. The most common kinds of activities for zoos are fund-raisers to care for or purchase a particular animal and fix up the habitats.

Many zoos or other wildlife-preservation organizations have "adopt-an-animal" programs. Adoptions usually start at about $25, so you may need to do some fund-raising. Here's an opportunity to involve the whole neighborhood, housing project, or school in adopting an animal. For more information about how you can help, the top; the lower hole should be about one-third of the way up from the bottom.

4. Put the wire through the top hole, running it along the inside of the carton and out the lower hole.

5. Make a bed for the bird with a clump of dried grass inside the carton.

6. Re-close the top of the carton and seal it tight with the packing tape.

7. Find a tree or wooden pole that's not too close to other trees or poles, or to buildings. Hammer the nails in about a foot apart, one above the other. Be sure the spot is well above the ground, high enough so people and animals can't get at the birds.

8. Hang the birdhouse by wrapping one end of the wire tightly around one nail and the other end of the wire around the other nail. Tug it a bit to make sure it will stay up.

❑ To build different kinds of birdhouses, write to Recycle for the Birds at the National Wildlife Federation; for information on taking care of birds, contact the National Audubon Society (see the resource section in Chapter 9).

contact your local zoo or the American Association of Zoological Parks and Aquariums (see Chapter 9).

Feed the Birds

It is estimated that if every fly egg produced a living fly that grew to maturity and reproduced, the world would be six feet deep in flies. Birds are the key to avoiding this prospect, since their diet consists mostly of bugs. Besides, they're pleasant to have around. By feeding the birds, you make sure they stick around. But don't worry, you won't interfere with their bug consumption. Here are a few ways to feed the birds:

❏ Take a bunch of unsalted peanuts still in the shell and tie them on a piece of yarn or string (no plastic or metal wire). Hang the string from a branch. The birds will find it. If you do this regularly, always in the same place(s), the birds will remember, and will come to visit often.

❏ Do the same thing with fruit rinds (orange, lemon, apple, melon, and so forth).

❏ Build or buy a bird feeder and keep it stocked with food.

❏ Scatter bird seed regularly in the same (safe) place.

Make a Birdbath

Birds need water as well as food, so another way to encourage them to visit is to provide a source of water for them in the form of a birdbath. Find a large, shallow ceramic or plastic pan (like the kind that sits beneath potted plants to catch excess water). Don't use metal, because it gets too hot in the summer and too cold in the winter for the birds to perch on. It should have a rim around the edge for the birds to sit on. Keep about two inches of water in the pan. Assign days for different people to clean and refill the birdbath. Put the pan up high, on a pedestal or ledge or in a tree, so no one bothers the birds.

Build a Rock Pile

Small mammals and reptiles, such as mice and lizards, like to hang out in nooks and crannies. Build a rock pile at least 4 feet wide and 2½ feet high for small mammals and reptiles to hide and rest in. Use varying sizes of rocks, leaving small gaps and nooks for the animals to hide in. Be sure to choose a location where the rock pile will not block any paths or be in anyone's way. Consult local authorities (game wardens, park rangers, fire departments, parents) to make sure your "mini-habitat" is safe and legal.

Create a Backyard Wildlife Habitat

You can have your own backyard—or some other space—declared an Official Backyard Wildlife Habitat by the National Wildlife Federation (NWF). Creating a wildlife habitat involves providing food, water, cover, and places for the animals to raise their young and, says the NWF, "is easy to achieve and beautiful to be around."

Find an appropriate spot—someone's backyard, a portion of the schoolyard that can be marked off, a section of a nearby park (with permission from authorities, of course), or a small donated parcel of land. Identify the habitat elements (food, water, cover, as listed in the previous paragraph) that already exist; consult local parks and recreation personnel, science teachers, local nature organizations, and the NWF for help. Plants that provide food—seeds, fruits, and nuts—are good for birds and squirrels, for example. A dense area of shrubbery or a rock pile could be useful. Water can be provided in many ways—a birdbath, small pool, or existing spring, stream, or pond. The NWF provides complete information, resources, and instructions; see the resource listings in Chapter 9 for contact information.

Save the Gorillas and Other Endangered Animals

Digit was one of the original group of gorillas studied by the late Dr. Dian Fossey, whose interactions with the endangered mountain gorillas were portrayed in the movie *Gorillas in the Mist*. It was partly through Dr. Fossey's work that we discovered that gorillas are smart and gentle and not the ferocious brutes we usually see in movies. Digit was killed by poachers, who cut off his hands to be sold as ashtrays. Dr. Fossey created the Digit Fund to help save Digit's kind. Not long afterward, she was murdered.

The Digit Fund is now called the Dian Fossey Gorilla Fund; you can make one-time donations or become a full-fledged member. Memberships are about $30, or about $10 for students. You receive a membership card, a year's subscription to the Digit Newsletter, and the official Digit Fund decal. When you send in your membership application, you can ask that the membership card and certificate be made out in the name of your entire group. You also receive information about the gorillas, writings by Dr. Fossey about them (especially Digit), and photos and pictures of them, including a picture of "your" gorilla.

Additional wildlife organizations have preservation programs for other animals. See the animal-care and wildlife resource section in Chapter 9 for information.

Adopt a Whale

The Pacific Whale Foundation and the American Cetacean Society have adoption programs for whales and dolphins similar to those for the gorillas. Adoptive "parents" receive an Adoption Certificate, a photograph of "their" whale, a detailed letter about the whale's activities, a map showing recent sightings, and a newsletter.

Set an Example

The best way to teach others to be respectful of animals is by example. Respect animals' homes and habitats, and be kind to all animals (yes, even bugs—liberate them instead of killing them, when possible). When you see an animal suffering, try to alleviate its pain. Don't engage in sports or activities that are cruel to animals.

8

Helpful Hints and General Information

By now you probably have some idea of the specific projects you want to undertake. The information in this chapter will help you find the ways and means of completing your projects. This information applies to many different activities and may need to be adapted slightly from one activity to another.

Collection Drives

Collection drives are a good way to gather lots of different kinds of stuff: recyclables, books, toys and games, clothes, blankets and towels, medicine, and just about anything else, including cash, depending on your project's needs. After collecting the items, you then need to sort and deliver them to an appropriate place or recipient—a recycling center or an individual, group, or institution.

It's important that every step, from collection to delivery, be carefully organized. You may need adult or older-teen volunteers to drive and help organize, but you can all collect, pack, sort, and clean the goods, and publicize the drive through flyers, public-service announcements, posters, and word-of-mouth.

What to Collect

What's collected will depend on the project's goal, the intended beneficiary of your efforts, what's available to be collected, and what resources are available for collection, transportation, and distribution. First you need to ask the intended recipients what they need and can accept. For example, if you're working with a women's shelter, they can probably use clothing for women and children, nonperishable foods, kitchen and toiletry items, bed and bath linens, blankets, and perhaps even furniture, bedding, appliances, and other larger items, depending on what the shelter officials tell you. Then you need to evaluate your people and resources to figure out what you can handle. For example, if you don't have trucks and drivers, you can't collect furniture.

Collecting

Collecting can be done door-to-door, at a drop-off site, or through some combination of the two. If you go door-to-door, you must be able to transport collected goods in some way: by car, cart, wagon, bicycle basket, backpack, and so forth.

Also make sure it's safe. When collecting door-to-door, don't go by yourself, and don't go into anyone's house. Wait outside the house, no matter what. If someone says he or she needs help carrying the item from inside, get the address and arrange to come back later with an adult. If the person won't agree to this, just thank him or her and leave without collecting anything. Plan your route beforehand and make sure someone knows it; let people know where you're going and when.

Drop-off collection is easier for the collectors, since it means the donors transport the goods. This method requires selected drop-off points, bins or other containers to hold the donated items, and attendants to receive (or reject, if necessary) and guard the donations. Make sure your drop-off points are safe, not in anyone's way, and open at convenient times.

For example, if you're conducting a collection drive at a school, get permission from school administrators to set up collection stations near the entrances, in the cafeteria, and outside where parents pick up and drop off their children. These drop-off points should be open about half an hour before and after school and during recess and lunch. Goods should be guarded or locked away between collection times. Wherever you put your drop-off points, whether in school or somewhere else, be sure to get permission from the people in charge of the location. Set a deadline for donations, make sure people know it, and stick to it. Otherwise things will dribble in for months.

Drop-off collections need more publicity, because people have to know about your collection drive and when and where they can drop items off. Use flyers, posters, PA announcements, bulletin-board notices, on-line announcements, and other advertising methods and materials to let people know about your collections. Be sure to include the following information:

❑ What you're collecting (be as specific as possible)
❑ How, where, and when you're collecting (specific dates, times, places)
❑ Why you're collecting it (for a homeless shelter, a hospital, and so forth)
❑ Whom to contact for more information
❑ Anything else donors need to know, such as directions to drop-off points, the name of your group, and so forth.

Assembling and Sorting

Once you've collected everything, gather it at one location for sorting, inspection, cleaning, and packing. This big sort will be easier if you do some initial work as you collect, such as rejecting or throwing away any donations that are unsuitable, too broken to repair, or too dirty to clean.

For a recycling drive, sort items according to the instructions from your recycling center. Clothing should be separated by size (adult, child, infant) and type (shirts, trousers, dresses). Everything should be cleaned—it would be less than generous to donate anything dirty. For clothing or linens, try to arrange for donated services—a volunteer's washing machine or donated or discounted services at a local laundromat or dry cleaner, for example. The same goes for repairs. Get volunteers or solicit donated services from appropriate repair shops.

Delivery and Distribution

Pack goods securely to avoid leakage and breaking. For shipping, follow postal regulations for packing method and materials. For delivery to a shelter, hospital, or other institution, make prior arrangements with the institution so that someone is there to receive your donation.

Transportation

You'll need transportation to haul goods from collection sites to the recycling center, institution, post office, or wherever they need to go. Recruit volunteers with suitable vehicles, and give them precise written instructions, directions, and schedules to follow.

Money

Some projects in this book can be done with no money at all, but many of them require the use of money in some way, whether it's getting your bus fare to visit someone or raising funds to build a community recycling center. If a project involves money, certain steps can be taken to ensure everything works out right. Money is complicated: cash, checks, receipts, accounts, interest, deposits, change. . . . Money can cause enormous trouble if you don't keep careful, accurate accounts and keep the money safe. If you have no significant experience in handling money (spending your allowance doesn't count), you may want to consult with someone who does.

Budgets and Goals

Before you begin a project, figure out what goods and services you need to complete it and how much they'll cost. Include such items as postage, photocopying, transportation, and any supplies and materials (including a notebook for tracking expenses). Add it up. Now you know how much you need to cover expenses. The final total you collect should exceed your expenses by a large margin—the larger, the better.

Fund-raising

This topic is too complex to cover here except to stress that there are several ways to raise money. The first thing you have to decide is what method(s) you're going to use. Are you going to sell things? What? How, when, and where—door-to-door, in front of the supermarket, at the flea market? Or are you just going to ask for donations? If so, the same questions apply: How, when, and where? What will you collect the money in—cans, boxes, old tennis shoes? The key factors to consider are:

- ❏ Feasibility: Can this be done given our resources, abilities, age, and so forth.
- ❏ Safety: Will we be exposing ourselves or others to danger or trouble?
- ❏ Effectiveness: Is it likely to yield good results?

Another option is to apply for grants, which are funds awarded by organizations or foundations for specific purposes. Many of the agencies listed in Chapter 9 offer grants or can tell you who does. Applying for grants is not difficult, but it does require a certain amount of knowledge and information—too much to include here. If this option interests you (and I recommend investigating it), there are many useful books and knowledgeable people you can consult.

The resource section includes several handbooks on raising funds, from bake sales to grant proposals. There's lots of help out there; you just have to do a little digging.

Storing Money

When collecting money, you need a secure place to store it. For example, if you're collecting money in canisters, make sure they have secure lids and that you can keep them somewhere safe, under lock and key. When you remove the money from the canisters, keep it in a strongbox, and find a safe place to keep the box and a reliable person to keep the key.

Keeping Accounts

There are two basic transactions in accounting:

❏ *Credits* are monies that come in, through donations or collections or sales. Credits get added to the total amount.

❏ *Debits* are the monies that go out, through spending or buying or loans. Debits are subtracted from the total.

At the end of each day, and at specified breaks during the day, count the money and write down the amounts in a notebook or ledger. Count the money twice, or have two people count it to avoid mistakes. Your written notes should indicate where each amount came from: Each entry should include the amount, where or who it came from, and the date it was received. If any money goes out to buy something or for some other reason, it gets subtracted from the total. These are your debits. Make clear, specific notes on them: the amount, who took it, when they took it, and what it's for. If you buy something, get a receipt and keep it with your money and accounts. Return change from purchases, and note that the change was returned, specifying how much, when it was returned, and who returned it.

The total amount collected, before subtracting any expenses or outgoing funds, is your *gross total*. The final total you get after subtracting total debits from the gross total is your *net total*, also called *net proceeds*. This will be the amount you end up with to donate or use.

If the project goes on for a while, you're going to need to keep track of all the money so that your accounts come out even at the end. That is, the amount left after figuring out all of your credits and debits should equal the total amount donated minus the amount spent. This amount is your net proceeds. If it's a long-term project, you may want to open a bank account in the name of the project and deposit all the money at the end of each day. The bank can tell you how to set up such an account. But even if you have the money in the bank, you still need to track deposits and withdrawals and balance the account according to the bank statement. A parent, teacher, or someone at the bank can teach you how to balance an account, which is a very useful skill to have.

Staying Balanced and Effective

Credits should far outweigh debits. If not, something's wrong:

❏ You're not collecting enough to cover your expenses: Collect more—work harder, put in longer hours, use different methods—and reassess your budget.
❏ You're not keeping expenses down, or you're spending money on unnecessary or irrelevant things: Reevaluate what you consider a legitimate project expense, and check to see where you can cut costs.
❏ You're not keeping close enough track of your money, allowing for loss, theft, and errors: Reevaluate your tracking and storage methods, be more careful, and perhaps get help.

There are several ways to avoid situations like these. As previously mentioned, make sure your budget is realistic, keep the money secure, and keep close, accurate accounts. *Never* make personal loans of any amount to anyone (including yourself) from project money—this is a sure recipe for trouble. Decide beforehand what constitutes a legitimate project expense for which you may use project funds, and be strict about it. Try to get as many goods and services donated as possible, for one of the marks of a successful service project is frugality. The smaller the percentage of expenditures, the more effective the project.

Checks, Money Orders, and Cashier's Checks

If you're collecting cash, it's a good idea to go to the bank and deposit it in a savings account or change it to a check, money order, or cashier's check as soon as possible. If you're donating the money, find out what name goes on the check, and then buy a money order or cashier's check (the bank can tell you how) with that name on it. Get the money to the person or organization as soon as possible, and get a receipt so you can prove you donated the money to the right person if anyone has any questions.

When dealing with money, it's best to get things done quickly and not let it sit around. The longer it sits around, the more likely it can get lost, stolen, mixed up, fought over, or forgotten.

Giving Wisely

If you plan to make a donation to a particular charity, check to ensure that your money will go to those in need and not to administrative expenses and executive salaries. For any charity or nonprofit organization, administrative expenses (salaries, overhead, fund-raising, and pubic relations) should constitute no more than 25 percent of the organization's budget, with at least 75 percent going to actual programs and services. The greater the ratio of program to administrative expenses, the better. Any organization that uses less than 75 percent of its money for programs and services may not use your contribution as you would like it to be used. You also need to check that your funds go to help your intended recipients with no political, religious, or other strings attached. To find out how a charity or nonprofit organization manages its funds, contact the following organizations:

❑ National Charities Information Bureau, 19 Union Square West, Sixth Floor, New York, NY 10003. This organization publishes *The Wise Giving Guide*, in which you can look up a charity and see how it rates.
❑ Council of Better Business Bureaus, Philanthropic Advisory Service, Suite 800, 4200 Wilson Blvd., Arlington, VA 22202, (703) 276-0100.

Publicity

There are two reasons to publicize your service activities. One is to let others know how they can help you. For example, if you're collecting Christmas-tree ornaments for a hospital, you need to let people know about it so they can bring the ornaments.

Another reason is to make sure people know what you're doing. Not only is this encouraging for you; it can also inspire other people. They might help you with your project or start something of their own. Either way it's fine, since the point is to get people to help in whatever way they can.

Publicity Methods

The main ingredients of any kind of publicity are an audience, a message, and a means of conveying the message. The methods you use will depend on what you want to say, your intended audience, and what resources you have (money, skills, people, materials, and so forth) for communicating. Some of the most common publicity methods are:

❏ Flyers and leaflets that can be passed out, mailed, e-mailed, or faxed

❏ News releases (pre-written articles) that can be delivered, mailed, e-mailed, or faxed to newspapers and radio and TV stations

❏ Public-service announcements delivered, mailed, e-mailed, or faxed to radio and TV stations so they can read them on the air

❏ Personal or mass-mailing letters, mailed, e-mailed, faxed, or delivered

❏ Announcements over the PA system

❏ Articles in newsletters and bulletins

❏ Advertisements

❏ Posters

❏ On-line announcements on computer bulletin boards.

Of course, there are the more exotic and costly stunts like sky-writing, blimps, and so on, but stick to the basics for now—save the placard-bearing elephants for later.

Many excellent books, manuals, and informational materials provide details about conducting publicity campaigns of all kinds. For information about how to get the word out, see Chapter 9's resource listings, and check your local library. Also check to see if anyone you know (parents, teachers, and so forth) has experience in this area and would be willing to help and/or instruct.

How to Get People, Businesses, and Others to Help Out

Your project could probably benefit from some kind of outside help, whether it's use of your parents' washing machine, a teacher's expertise, store-donated prizes for a raffle, photocopying services from the local copy shop, or just plain cash. Just remember that whether you're asking your goofy Uncle Ed or the CEO of General Motors, both are still just people.

There are three basic reasons why people will help you. First, because you're promoting a good cause. Second, they like you and your attitude. And third, you look like you have your act together, so you won't waste their time, effort, and contributions. Whether you get the help you want will depend on some combination of these three factors, so you need to cover all three bases.

To address the first factor, determine whether the people you want to approach are likely to be sympathetic to your cause. The answer will usually be yes, but don't take anything for granted. Have some information available about your cause and why it's important. Hard facts (numbers, specifics) are often helpful: "There are about 700 homeless people in our town, and only three shelters to serve them, so you can imagine how overwhelmed these shelters are." Do some research.

For factor number two, be cheerful and enthusiastic about what you're doing. Enthusiasm is contagious, and people will often get caught up in your excitement. After all, if you're not excited about your own project, why should they get worked up about it? Sincere belief in the worth of what you're doing will be a prime factor in persuading others to lend their support.

No matter who you're dealing with (even your own parents and siblings), always observe the utmost courtesy and respect. Smile, say "please" and "thank you," and generally mind your manners. Remember, they don't *have to* help you. Even if people respond rudely, keep your cool. You're not responsible for their behavior, only yours.

Part of good manners is respect for other people's time, which brings us to factor three. If you're disorganized, you'll probably end up wasting time and making a bad impression. Before you approach people, make sure you know what you want from them, how much, when you want it, and why. Write up a basic fact sheet about your project, including what it is, who benefits, what's needed to complete it, and who people can contact for more information. (It's a good idea to do this anyway, since it helps you clarify your ideas for yourself.)

In some cases—depending on the scale of your project and the level of help you're requesting—you may want to send a letter. Be sure to address it to the proper person: Get names and addresses of managers and officials to whom you intend to appeal. This letter should be no longer than one side of one page, typed, and should be in correct letter format (check secretarial handbooks or ask someone). Explain your project and how the person can help. Close by thanking him or her and letting that person know you'll be calling or visiting soon (and then do so).

When dealing with a store, restaurant, or business of some kind, ask to speak to the manager. Sometimes clerks or secretaries will ask you why you want to speak to the manager: Part of their job is to keep people from wasting their boss's time. Tell them it's about a community-service project, and hand over any materials you may have—fact sheets, flyers, and so forth. If you've already sent a letter, let them know this.

Once you have the ear of whoever makes the decisions, be as concise, clear, and courteous as possible. Smile and be cheerful and confident. Briefly explain your project and the role you see them playing in it. Ask for what you would like from them politely but directly. Be prepared to negotiate: They may not be able to give you exactly what you asked for, but they still may be able to offer something useful. Be flexible, but keep your objectives in mind. If you're asking for money, ask for a specific amount and let them know why you need it. Have a rough budget ready so they can see how the money will be used.

Be prepared to answer questions about the project. Be persuasive and determined but not pushy or loud. No matter what the result of your meeting is, be sure to thank the other person for his or her time.

Credit Where Credit Is Due

No project completes itself. It takes people to make it work. Inevitably, thanks will be called for. If you completed a project by yourself, thanks are not an issue. But most projects will involve someone else, even if only for advice and moral support. Here are some ways of acknowledging everyone's contribution.

Thank Your Helpers

People always like to know their efforts are appreciated, so always make sure you let your helpers know how grateful you are.

If a person, store, or organization helps your project by giving time, money, goods, or services, be sure to thank all of them. If your little sister fed your dog while you collected cans, she gets a thank-you. If the president of Paramount Studios let you use a picture from one of their movies to promote your project, he or she gets a thank-you, too. Make a list of everyone who helped you to make sure you're not leaving anyone out.

In some cases it may be enough to just say "thank you," but most of the time it's best to write a note, make a card, or create a sign or plaque, and somehow make it an "official" thank-you (see box below). Not only is it basic good manners, it also creates good relationships so that if you need help in the future, someone who feels appreciated is likely to give it.

Ways to Say "Thank You"

❏ Write a note:

Dear Ms. Bertola,

Thank you for helping us sew the Christmas stockings for the homeless shelter. The shelter was very happy to receive them, and we couldn't have done it without you.

Affectionately,

George Laws, Sandra Poe, Livia Sarkesian, and Chinua Matthews.

Make it neat, clear, and pleasing to look at. Use attractive stationery, store-bought or homemade.

❏ Make or buy a thank-you card, and write something similar to the above note inside the card.

❏ Make a poster or certificate:

The Blueberry Hill Youth Alliance
wishes to thank
Quang Vo's Mini Mart
for invaluable contributions to the cause of
helping the elderly in our neighborhood.
April 1995

You can buy pre-printed certificates and fill them in, or design and decorate your own. In either case, make it look special and official,

For example, if a store or shop donated something to your project, whether it's an actual thing (food, blankets, prizes) or a service (photocopying, printing, advice and instruction)—make a sign, certificate, or poster that the store manager can hang on the wall for all to see. If a parent, teacher, relative, friend, or other individual helped out, buy or make a thank-you card.

something a merchant would be proud to hang on his or her wall. This doesn't mean it has to look slick, just well-crafted and sincere.

❑ If your funds allow, a small but meaningful gift is a good way to show appreciation. A note or card should accompany the gift, with a note similar to the one above. It's important to keep it small, since it makes people wonder how wisely the project money is being used if they receive an elaborate gift—unless it's donated. If this is the case, be sure it's indicated on the accompanying note:

Dear Mr. Sabetan,
Please accept this token of our appreciation for your help in our recycling drive. The enclosed dinner-for-two coupons were graciously donated by Scott's Seafood. We hope you enjoy them.
Sincerely yours,
Mr. Carlyle's Social Studies Class
McChesney Junior High

❑ Thank your helpers in any written or spoken announcements associated with the project. For example, if you're presenting a check before an audience, be sure to mention your helpers by name: "This donation wouldn't have been possible without the help of Stuart's Records and Ms. Kowalski from Salinger High School." The same goes for any media coverage you receive. If your project is a display or artwork of some kind, be sure to include a visible placard or legend.

Thank Yourselves

As we said before, people like to know their efforts are appreciated, and you're no exception. Make sure people know that you're responsible for the projects you do. Whenever you do a project, try to include a sign, note, card, or some kind of message that lets people know who did the project.

For one thing, it's a reminder for whomever you're helping that someone—a real person or group with a name—cares about them. If you're in the hospital, for example, and you read a scrapbook of funny stories and jokes made by a group of kids, you want to know who created it. A note that says "This book was put together by the Lockwood Gardens Service Gang" creates a personal touch. Also, some people may want to thank you, so they'll want to know who you are.

Celebrate Success

When a project is over, give yourselves a pat on the back! Have a party, go out for pizza, buy yourselves ice cream, or just give yourselves a big hurrah. Do something to celebrate. You deserve it!

9

Resources:

Who to Call,

Where to Write,

What to Read

The organizations and materials listed here are a starting point, not a definitive directory. You may be able to work directly with some of these organizations; many of them will refer you to agencies in your area with which you must then get in touch. In most cases, these listings will just get you started, and you will need to make a few more calls or get more materials or referrals. Your local library may have some of the publications listed here, or it may have different but equally helpful materials. Check your phone book, library, and other sources for local agencies and publications.

Organizations

General Service and the Poor and Homeless

- ❑ American Red Cross, 430 17th St. NW, Washington, DC 20006, (202) 737-8300. Provides emergency services and life-saving skills.
- ❑ Americorp, (800) 94-ACORP or 942-2677. President Clinton's national service initiative; includes VISTA and various state and local programs nationwide.
- ❑ The Box Project, P.O. Box 435, Plainville, CT 06062, (203) 747-8182. "Sister family" program to help needy families; scholarships.
- ❑ Campus Outreach Opportunity League (COOL), 1511 K St. NW, Suite 307, Washington, DC 20005, (202) 637-7004. College student involvement in community service nationwide.
- ❑ Catholic Network of Volunteer Service, 4121 Harewood Rd., NE, Washington, DC 20017, (202) 529-1100 or (800) 543-5046. Matches volunteers and needy projects.
- ❑ Catholic Relief Services, 209 West Fayette St., Baltimore, MD 21201-3403, (410) 625-2220 or (800) 235-2772. Food and care for the needy all over the world, regardless of religious affiliation.
- ❑ Child Health Foundation, 10630 Little Patuxent Pkwy., Suite 325, Columbia, MD 21044, (301) 596-4514. Child poverty around the world.
- ❑ Christmas in April U.S.A., 1225 Eye St., NW, Suite 600, Washington, DC 20005, (202) 326-8268 or (800) 473-4229. Home renovation for low-income families and individuals.

❏ Corporation for National Service, 1201 New York Ave., 8th floor, Washington, DC 20525, (202) 606-5000 or (800) 942-2677. Volunteers in Service to America (VISTA) and Student Community Service (SCS) programs.

❏ Do Something, P.O. Box 2409 JAF, New York, NY 10116, (212) 527-5700. Helps young people to carry out service projects in their communities through grants and technical assistance.

❏ Families International, 11700 W. Lake Park Dr., Milwaukee, WI 53224, (414) 359-1040. Family services.

❏ Four-One-One, 7304 Beverly St., Annandale, VA 22003, (703) 354-6270. National clearinghouse on volunteerism.

❏ Good Bears of the World, P.O. Box 13097, Toledo, OH 43613, (419) 531-5365. Teddy bears delivered to institutionalized children and adults.

❏ Habitat for Humanity International, 121 Habitat St., Americus, GA 31709-3498, (912) 924-6935 or (800)/HABITAT. Home construction and repair for low-income families and individuals.

❏ Heifer Project International, P.O. Box 808, Little Rock, AR 72203, (501) 376-6836 or (800) 422-0474. Livestock for poor countries and for needy rural Americans.

❏ The Hope Foundation, P.O. Box 560908, Dallas, TX 75247, (214) 630-5765 or (800) 843-4073. Helps homeless kids stay in school.

❏ Junior League, 660 First Ave., New York, NY 10016-3241, (212) 683-1515. Ideas, referrals.

❏ Love Letters, P.O. Box 416875, Chicago, IL 60641, (708) 620-1970 or (708) 515-9501. Letters and cards to sick children.

❏ National Association of Community Action Agencies, 1775 T St., NW, First Floor., Washington, DC 20009, (202) 265-7546. Low-income housing, economic development, employment and training programs, Head Start, senior programs.

❏ National Student Campaign Against Hunger and Homelessness, 11965 Venice Blvd., #408, Los Angeles, CA 90066, (310) 397-5270, ext. 324.

❏ Prison Pen Pals, Box 1217, Cincinnati, OH 45201 (include SASE).

❏ Project HOPE, Carter Hall, Millwood, VA 22646, (703) 837-2100 or (800) 544-4673. Child health and well-being worldwide.

❏ Project Service Leadership, 2034 NE 104th, Seattle, WA 98125, (206) 524-1434. Assistance in developing service projects.

❏ Retired Senior Volunteer Program (RSVP), 1125 Quintara St., San Francisco, CA 94116, (415) 731-3335. Volunteer opportunities for seniors.

❏ Salvation Army, P.O. Box 269, Alexandria, VA 22313, (703) 684-5500.

❑ Second Harvest National Food Bank Network, 116 S. Michigan Ave., Suite 4, Chicago, IL 60603, (312) 263-2303 or (800) 771-2303. National network of food banks.

❑ United Way of America, 701 N. Fairfax St., Alexandria, VA 22314, (703) 836-7100. Funding for a wide variety of charitable projects.

❑ USA Harvest, P.O. Box 628, Louisville, KY 40201-1628, (800) USA-4-FOOD (872-4366) or (502) 583-7756. Collection and distribution of food for homeless shelters, food banks, and soup kitchens (no money accepted, only time, materials, or food).

❑ Veterans of Foreign Wars of the U.S., Voluntary Service, 200 Maryland Ave. NE, Washington, DC 20002, (202) 233-4110. Volunteer clearinghouse for those who wish to help veterans.

❑ VISTA (Volunteers in Service to America). See Corporation for National Service.

❑ Youth Service America, 1101 15th St. NW, Suite 200, Washington, DC 20005, (202) 296-2994.

Disabilities, Illnesses, and Health

❑ AIDS. See Centers for Disease Control.

❑ Alcoholics Anonymous, Box 459, Grand Central Station, New York, NY 10163, (212) 686-1100. Can also refer to Al-Anon for families of alcoholics and Alateen for teens with alcohol problems or in alcoholic homes.

❑ American Academy of Child and Adolescent Psychiatry, 3615 Wisconsin Ave. NW, Washington, DC 20016, (202) 966-7300. Services for disabled children and adolescents.

❑ American Academy of Pediatrics, P.O. Box 927, 141 NW Point Blvd., Elk Grove Village, IL 60009, (708) 228-5005. Information, referrals, and services to children and youth.

❑ American Association for Rehabilitation Therapy, P.O. Box 93, North Little Rock, AR 72116. Information and services for professionals and disabled people.

❑ American Association for the Advancement of Science, Project on Science, Technology, and Disability, 1333 H St. NW, Washington, DC 20005, (202) 326-6630. Assistance with improving access to science programs for students with disabilities.

❏ American Camping Association, 5000 State Rd. 67N, Martinsville, IN 46151, (317) 342-8456. Information and referrals on outdoor excursions for disabled people.

❏ American Cancer Society, 1599 Clifton Rd. NE, Atlanta, GA 30329, (404) 320-3333.

❏ American Council of the Blind, 1155 15th St., NW, Suite 720, Washington, DC 20005, (202) 467-5081 or (800) 424-8666.

❏ American Foundation for Technology Assistance, Route 14, Box 230, Morganton, NC 28655, (704) 438-9697. Products, information, and funding for disabled people with special technology needs.

❏ American Heart Association, 7320 Greenville Ave., Dallas, TX 75231, (214) 750-5300.

❏ American Lung Association, 1740 Broadway, New York, NY 10019, (212) 315-8700.

❏ American Red Cross. See "General Service and Volunteers."

❏ American Rehabilitation Counseling Association, 5999 Stevenson Ave., Alexandria, VA 22304, (703) 823-9800 or (800) 347-6647.

❏ American Self-Help Clearinghouse, St. Clare's Community Mental Health Center, Denville, NJ 07834, (201) 625-7101 or (800) 367-6274. Referrals to self-help groups and assistance for starting self-help and support groups.

❏ Amytrophic Lateral Sclerosis Association, 21021 Ventura Blvd., Suite 321, Woodland Hills, CA 91364, (818) 340-7500.

❏ Association for Retarded Citizens, 500 E. Border, Suite 300, Arlington, TX 76010, (817) 261-6003. Services for mentally retarded adults and children.

❏ Blinded American Veterans Foundation, P.O. Box 65900, Washington, DC 20035-5900, (202) 462-4430 or (800) 242-0161.

❏ Centers for Disease Control (CDC) National AIDS Hotline: (800) 342-AIDS (2437). For Spanish, call (800) 344-SIDA (7432); and for TDD (for the hearing impaired) call (800) 243-7833. AIDS information; referrals to AIDS programs and organizations in your area.

❏ COMPEER, Inc., 259 Monroe Ave., Suite B-1, Rochester, NY 14607, (716) 546-8280 or (800) 836-0475. Support and companionship for the mentally ill.

❏ Disabled American Veterans, 3725 Alexandria Pike, Cold Spring, KY 41076, (606) 441-7300, or 807 Main Ave., SW, Washington, DC 20024, (202) 554-3501.

❏ Epilepsy Foundation of America, 4351 Garden City Dr., Landover, MD 20785, (301) 459-3700 or (800) EFA-1000 (332-1000).

❑ Estate Planning for the Disabled, 3100 Arapahoe Ave., #112, Boulder, CO 30303, (209) 239-7558 or (800) 683-4607. Assistance in setting up financial planning for children with special needs.

❑ Extensions for Independence, 555 Saturn Blvd., San Diego, CA 92154, (619) 423-7709. Products for the visually handicapped.

❑ Federation for Children with Special Needs, P.O. Box 992, Westfield, MA 02116, (617) 482-2915.

❑ Federation of the Handicapped, 211 W. 14th St., New York, NY 10011, (212) 206-4321.

❑ Foundation for Children with Learning Disabilities, 99 Park Ave., New York, NY 10016, (212) 687-7211.

❑ Foundation for Science and the Handicapped, 154 Julian Ct., Clarendon Hills, IL 60514, (708) 323-4181. Advocacy and educational services.

❑ Gazette International Networking Institute, 5100 Oakland Ave., #206, St. Louis, MO 63110, (314) 534-0475. Information on living with the effects of polio.

❑ Goodwill Industries of America, 9200 Wisconsin Ave., Bethesda, MD 20814, (301) 530-6500. Services and opportunities for people with disabilities and special needs.

❑ Handicapped Advocacy Alliance, 918 Southland, Lansing, MI 48910, (517) 393-0305. Advocacy and referrals for the disabled.

❑ Handicapped Business Specialty Center, Lansing Community College, Lansing, MI 48901, (517) 484-8440. Information and referrals.

❑ Handicapped Education Services, Wayne State University, 583 Student Center Building, Detroit MI 48202, (313) 577-1851. Educational and information services.

❑ HEATH Resource Center, One Dupont Circle, Suite 800, Washington, DC 20036, (202) 939-9329 or (800) 544-3284. Information about college education for the disabled.

❑ The Housing Center, University of Maryland Center for Mental Health, 645 W. Redwood St., Baltimore, MD 21201, (410) 328-6669. Housing for the mentally ill.

❑ International Council on Disability, 25 E. 21st St., New York, NY 10010, (212) 420-1500. International programs for disabled people.

❑ International Foundation for Stutterers, P.O. Box 462, Belle Mead, NJ 08502, (201) 359-6469.

❑ Learning Disabilities Network, 25 Accord Park Dr., Rockland, MA 02370, (617) 982-8100.

❑ Learning Disabilities of America Association, 4156 Library Rd., Pittsburgh, PA 15234, (412) 341-1515. Information and referrals.

❑ Learning How, P.O. Box 35481, Charlotte, NC 28227, (704) 376-4735. Support and self-esteem building for disabled people.

❑ Life Development Institute, 1720 E. Monte Vista, Phoenix, AZ 85006, (602) 254-0822. Programs for adults with learning disabilities.

❑ Life Centers for the Handicapped, 352 Park Ave. S., New York, NY 10010, (212) 532-6740. Care for handicapped whose families cannot care for them.

❑ Little People of America, P.O. Box 9897, Washington, DC 20016, (301) 589-0730. Assistance for people of short stature.

❑ Marin Puzzle People, 17 Buena Vista Ave., Mill Valley, CA 94941, (415) 383-8763. Services for learning-disabled adults.

❑ MedEscort International, ABE International Airport, P.O. Box 8766, Allentown, PA 18105, (215) 791-3111 or (800) 255-7182. Travel escorts for children and disabled people.

❑ The Names Project Foundation, 2362 Market St., San Francisco, CA 94114, (415) 882-5500. Memorial quilt project to help people with AIDS.

❑ National Alliance for the Mentally Ill, 200 N. Glebe Rd., Suite 1015, Arlington, VA 22203 (703) 524-7600. Advocacy and services.

❑ National Association for Down's Syndrome, P.O. Box 4542, Oak Brook, IL 60522, (708) 325-9112.

❑ National Association of the Deaf, 814 Thayer Ave., Silver Spring, MD 20910, (301) 587-1788 (for hearing and hearing impaired callers). Services for the deaf; public education about deafness.

❑ National Ataxia Foundation, 15500 Wayzata Blvd., #750, Wayzata, MN 55391, (612) 473-7666.

❑ National Center for Family-Centered Care, 7910 Woodmont Ave., Suite 300, Bethesda, MD 20814, (301) 654-6549. Family-centered approach to caring for special-needs children.

❑ National Center for Youth with Disabilities, University of Minnesota, Box 721-UMHC, Minneapolis, MN 55455, (612) 626-2825.

❑ National Chronic Pain Outreach Association, 7979 Old Georgetown Rd., Suite 100, Bethesda, MD 20814, (301) 652-4948.

❑ National Clearinghouse of Rehabilitation and Training Materials, Oklahoma State University, 115 Old USDA Bldg., Stillwater, OK 74078, (405) 624-7650.

❑ National Clearinghouse on Women and Girls with Disability, Educational Equity Concepts, Inc., 114 E. 32nd St., New York, NY 10016, (212) 725-1803.

❑ National Council on Independent Living, Fourth St. & Broadway, Troy, NY 12180, (518) 274-1979. Independent living for disabled people.

❏ National Hemophilia Foundation, The Soho Bldg., 110 Greene St., New York, NY 10012, (212) 219-8180.

❏ National Hospice Organization, 1901 No. Moore St., Suite 901, Arlington, VA 22209, (703) 243-5900 or (800) 658-8898. Hospice referral and information services.

❏ National Information Center for Children and Youth with Disabilities, P.O. Box 1492, Washington, DC 20013, (703) 893-6061 or (800) 999-5599.

❏ National Institute of Mental Health, 5600 Fishers Ln., Rockville, MD 20852, (301) 443-4513.

❏ National Kidney Foundation, 2233 Wisconsin Ave. NW, Washington, DC 20007, (202) 337-6600.

❏ National Leadership Coalition on AIDS, 1730 M St., NW, Suite 905, Washington, DC 20036, (202) 429-0930.

❏ National Maternal and Child Health, 38th and R Sts. NW, Washington, DC 20057, (800) 346-2742.

❏ National Medical Center Children's Hospital, 111 Michigan Ave. NW, Washington, DC 20010, (202) 745-5000.

❏ National Multiple Sclerosis Society, 205 E. 42nd St., New York, NY 10017, (212) 986-3240 or (800) 624-8236.

❏ National Network for the Learning Disabled, 808 N. 82nd St., Suite F2, Scottsdale, AZ 85257, (602) 941-5112.

❏ National Organization for Rare Disorders, P.O. Box 8923, New Fairfield, CT 06812, (203) 746-6518 or (800) 999-6673.

❏ National Organization on Disability, 910 16th St. NW, Suite 600, Washington, DC 20006, (202) 293-5960 or (800) 248-ABLE (2253).

❏ National Rehabilitation Information, 8455 Colesville Rd., Suite 935, Silver Spring, MD 20910, (301) 588-4633.

❏ Orton Dyslexia Society, 724 York Rd., Baltimore, MD 21204, (301) 296-0232 or (800) ABCD-123 (222-3123).

❏ Parents Helping Parents, 535 Race St., San Jose, CA 95126, (408) 288-5010. Information, referrals, and programs for families with special-needs children.

❏ People-to-People Committee for the Handicapped, P.O. Box 18131, Washington, DC 20036, (301) 774-7446. International programs.

❏ Perceptions Inc., P.O. Box 142, Millburn, NJ 07041, (201) 376-3766. Information and referrals for the disabled.

❏ Phoenix Project, P.O. Box 84151, Seattle, WA 98124, (206) 329-1371. Information about head injuries.

❏ Recording for the Blind, 20 Roszel Rd., Princeton, NJ 08540, (609) 452-0606. To order books call (800) 221-4792.

❏ Rehabilitation International, 25 E. 21st St., New York, NY 10010, (212) 420-1500.

❏ Rehabilitation R&D Center, VA Medical Center, 3801 Miranda Ave., 153, Palo Alto, CA 94304.

❏ Rehabilitation Services Administration, 330 C St. SW, Washington, DC 20202, (202) 732-1362.

❏ Ronald McDonald House, Kroc Dr., Oak Brook, IL 60521, (708) 575-7418. Temporary lodgings for sick children undergoing treatment.

❏ Services to Advance Independent Living, 1700 S. First Ave., Suite 100, Yuma, AZ 85364, (602) 783-3308.

❏ Sibling Information Network, 1776 Ellington Rd., S. Windsor, CT 06074, (203) 648-1205. Help for siblings and family members of disabled people.

❏ Siblings for Significant Change, 105 E. 22nd St., New York, NY 10010, (212) 420-0776. Support for siblings of disabled people.

❏ Technical Assistance for Special Populations Program, University of Illinois, 345 Education Bldg., 1310 S. Sixth, Champaign, IL 61820, (217) 333-0807.

❏ Time Out to Enjoy, P.O. Box 1084, Evanston, IL 60204, (312) 940-9633. Information and support for learning disabled adults.

❏ United Cerebral Palsy Associations, 7 Penn Plaza, Suite 804, New York, NY 10001, (212) 268-6655) or (800) 872-1827.

❏ Very Special Arts, JFK Center for the Performing Arts, Washington, DC 20566, (202) 662-8899. Arts programs for the disabled.

❏ World Institute on Disability, 510 16th St., Suite 100, Oakland, CA 94612, (510) 763-4100.

❏ Young Adult Institute, 460 W. 34th St., New York, NY 10001, (212) 563-7474. Services for disabled children and adults.

Education, Counseling, and Alliance Building

❏ American Association for the Advancement of Science. See "Disabilities, Illnesses, and Health."

❏ American Self-Help Clearinghouse. See "Disabilities, Illnesses, and Health."

❏ Anti-Defamation League, 823 UN Plaza, New York, NY 10017, (212) 490-2525. Multicultural education.

❏ Big Brothers/Big Sisters of America, 230 No. 13th St., Philadelphia, PA, 19107, (215) 567-7000. Mentorship and guidance services for inner-city and troubled youth.

❏ Character Education Partnership, 1250 N. Pitt St., Alexandria, VA 22314, (703) 739-9515. Consortium of educational associations and professionals providing referrals and information.

❏ Foundation for Children with Learning Disabilities. See "Disabilities, Illnesses, and Health."

❏ The Hope Foundation. See "General Service and the Poor and Homeless."

❏ Josephson Institute of Ethics, 310 Washington Blvd., Marina del Rey, CA 90292, (310) 306-1868. Program called "Character Counts," for character and moral development.

❏ Learning Disabilities Network. See "Disabilities, Illnesses, and Health."

❏ Learning Disabilities of America Association. See "Disabilities, Illnesses, and Health."

❏ Literacy Volunteers of America, Inc., 5795 Widewaters Pkwy., Syracuse, NY 13214-1846, (800) 228-8813 or (315) 445-8000. Literacy and English as a Second Language instruction programs.

❏ Life Development Institute. See "Disabilities, Illnesses, and Health."

❏ Marin Puzzle People. See "Disabilities, Illnesses, and Health."

❏ National Association for Mediation in Education, 205 Hampshire House, Box 33635, University of Massachusetts, Amherst, MA 01003-3635, (413) 545-2462. Peer mediation; conflict resolution.

❏ National Conference of Christians and Jews, 71 Fifth Ave., New York, NY 10003, (212) 206-0006. Multicultural education and materials.

❏ National Home Study Council, 1601 18th St. NW, Washington, DC 20009, (202) 234-5100. Information and quality control for correspondence education.

❏ National Network for the Learning Disabled. See "Disabilities, Illnesses, and Health."

❏ National Youth Leadership Council, 1910 W. County Rd. B, St. Paul, MN 55113, (612) 631-3672 or (800) FON-NYLC (366-6952). Information; referrals on a wide variety of youth educational, counseling, and mediation programs.

❏ Orton Dyslexia Society. See "Disabilities, Illnesses, and Health."

❏ Parents Helping Parents. See "Disabilities, Illnesses and Health."

❏ Quest International, P.O. Box 566, Granville, OH 43023, (614) 522-6400 or (800) 837-2801. Life skills and developmental education for youth (peer counseling, conflict resolution, and so forth).

❏ Sasha Bruce Youthwork, 1022 Maryland Ave. NW, Washington, DC 20002, (202) 675-9340. Life-skills counseling, shelters, recreation, and youth programs.

❏ Self Evaluation Consultants, P.O. Box 110, Evanston, IL 60204, (708) 492-0123. Anti-prejudice materials and programs.

❏ Time Out to Enjoy. See "Disabilities, Illnesses, and Health."

❏ TODOS, 678 13th St., Ste. 103, Oakland, CA 94612, (510) 444-6448. "Unlearning" prejudice and oppression; promoting multiculturalism.

❏ United Nations, United Nations Plaza, New York, NY 10017, (212) 963-1234.

❏ United Nations Associations of the USA, 485 Fifth Ave., New York, NY 10017, (212) 697-3232.

❏ Very Special Arts. See "Disabilities, Illnesses, and Health."

❏ The Virtues Project, 192 Sun Eagle Dr., RRI, Ganges, BC, Canada, V0S 1E0, (604) 537-4647. Character development.

Children and Youth

For most disabled, ill, homeless, or other specific child and youth services (for example, AIDS; literacy), check the appropriate category; many but not all are cross-referenced here.

❏ American Academy of Child and Adolescent Psychiatry. See "Disabilities, Illnesses, and Health."

❏ American Academy of Pediatrics. See "Disabilities, Illnesses, and Health."

❏ Big Brothers/Big Sisters of America. See "Education, Counseling, and Alliance Building."

❏ Campus Outreach Opportunity League (COOL). See "General Service and the Poor and Homeless."

❏ Children's Defense Fund, 25 E St., NW, Washington, DC 20001, (202) 628-8787. Various child and youth issues.

❏ Covenant House, 460 W. 41st St., New York, NY 10036, (212) 613-0300; hotline is (800) 999-9999, but should not be used, except in emergencies. Runaway shelters and assistance.

❏ Do Something. See "General Service and the Poor and Homeless."

❏ Federation for Children with Special Needs. See "Disabilities, Illnesses, and Health."

❏ Foundation for Children with Learning Disabilities. See "Disabilities, Illnesses, and Health."

❏ The Hope Foundation: see "General Service and the Poor and Homeless."

❏ MedEscort International. See "Disabilities, Illnesses, and Health."

❏ National Adoption Center, 1218 Chestnut St., Philadelphia, PA 19107, (215) 925-0200.

❏ National Association for Child Care Resource and Referral Agency (NACRA), 1319 F St. NW, Suite 606, Washington, DC, 20004, (202) 393-5501. Refers you to the child-care referral agency in your area.

❏ National Center for Missing and Exploited Children, 2101 Wilson Blvd., Suite 550, Arlington, VA 22201 (703) 235-3900; hotline is (800) 843-5678.

❏ National Center for Youth with Disability. See "Disabilities, Illnesses, and Health."

❏ National Information Center for Children and Youth with Disabilities. See "Disabilities, Illnesses, and Health."

❏ National Maternal and Child Health. See "Disabilities, Illnesses, and Health."

❏ National Network of Runaway and Youth Services, 1319 F St. NW, Suite 401, Washington, DC 20004, (202) 783-7949.

❏ National Youth Leadership Council. See "Education, Counseling, and Alliance Building."

❏ Quest International. See "Education, Counselling, and Alliance Building."

❏ Ronald McDonald Children's Charities, Kroc Dr., Oak Brook, IL 60521, (708) 575-7418.

❏ Sasha Bruce Youthwork. See "Education, Counselling, and Alliance Building."

❏ UNICEF, 333 East 38th St., New York, NY 10016, (212) 686-5522. Organization for helping children all over the world with food, clothing, education, medical care.

❏ U.S. Department of Health and Human Services, Administration for Children, Youth and Families, 330 C St. SW, Switzer Bldg., Washington, DC 20201, (202) 205-8347.

❏ Young Adult Institute. See "Disabilities, Illnesses, and Health."

❏ Youth Development, P.O. Box 178408, San Diego, CA 92177-8408, (619) 292-5683 or (800) HIT-HOME (448-4663). Assistance for runaways and abandoned children.

❏ Youth Service America. See "General Service and the Poor and Homeless."

Seniors

For most disabled, ill, homeless, or other specific senior services, check the appropriate category; many but not all are cross-referenced here.

- [ ] Aging in America, 1500 Pelham Parkway South, Bronx, NY 10461, (212) 824-4004. Research and services for gerontology professionals.
- [ ] American Association for International Aging, 1511 K St. NW, Suite 443, Washington, DC 20005, (202) 638-6815. Improving socioeconomic conditions for the elderly in developing countries.
- [ ] American Association of Homes for the Aging, 1129 20th St. NW, Washington, DC 20036, (202) 296-5960.
- [ ] Center for Understanding Aging, Framingham State College, Framingham, MA 01701, (508) 626-4979.
- [ ] Children of Aging Parents, 2761 Trenton Rd., Livittown, PA 19056, (215) 945-6900.
- [ ] Elder Care Locator, 1112 16th St. NW, Suite 100, Washington, DC 20036, (800) 677-1116. Helps find programs and organizations in your area that help the elderly.
- [ ] International Senior Citizens Association, 1102 S. Crenshaw Blvd., Los Angeles, CA 90019, (213) 857-6434.
- [ ] Magic Me, 2521 N. Charles St., Baltimore, MD 21201, (410) 243-9066. Friendships between young and old people.
- [ ] National Association of Area Agencies on Aging, 1112 16th St. NW, Suite 100, Washington, DC 20036, (202) 296-8130.
- [ ] National Council on the Aging, 409 Third St. SW, Second Floor, Washington, DC 20024, (202) 479-1200 or (800) 424-9046.
- [ ] Retired Senior Volunteer Program (RSVP). See "General Service and the Poor and Homeless."

Recycling and the Environment

- [ ] Alliance for Community Trees, 201 Lathrop Way, Suite F. Sacramento, CA 95815, (800) ACT-8886 (228-8886). Urban forestry.
- [ ] The Energy Efficiency and Renewable Energy Clearinghouse, P.O. Box 3048, Merrisfield, VA 22116, (800) 523-2929. Energy and conservation information packets.

❏ Cultural Survival, 46 Brattly St., Cambridge, MA 02138, (617) 621-3818. Information and activities about the rain forest and its inhabitants.

❏ Environmental Defense Fund, 257 Park Ave. S., New York, NY 10010, (212) 505-2100 or (800) 225-5333.

❏ Environmental Industries Association, 4301 Connecticut Ave. NW, Suite 300, Washington, DC 20008, (202) 244-4700. Free recycling of educational materials.

❏ Environmental Protection Agency, 401 M St. SW, Washington, DC 20460, (202) 260-4454. General environmental information; Earth Day.

❏ Freshwater Foundation, 725 County Road Six, Wayzata, MN 55391, (612) 471-9773. Informational materials and activity suggestions about keeping our water clean.

❏ Global Releaf, American Forests, P.O. Box 2000, Washington, DC 20013, (202) 667-3300 or (800) 368-5748. Tree planting.

❏ Greenpeace USA, 1436 U St., NW, Washington, DC 20007, (202) 462-1177. Information and activity suggestions for a wide variety of environmental and wildlife concerns.

❏ International Center for Development Policy, New Forests Project, 731 Eighth St. SE, Washington, DC 20003, (202) 547-3800. Tree planting.

❏ Izaak Walton League of America, 707 Conservation Lane, Gaithersburg, MD 20878, (301) 548-0150. Water conservation.

❏ Keep America Beautiful, 9 W. Broad St., Stamford, CT 06902, (203) 323-8987. Information; curricula; youth programs.

❏ Mothers & Others for a Livable Planet, 40 W. 20th St., New York, NY 10011, (212) 242-0010. Information on "green" products, housekeeping, foods, and so forth; publishes *The Green Guide for Everyday Living*.

❏ Natural Resources Defense Council, 40 W. 20th St., New York, NY 10011, (212) 727-2700.

❏ National Arbor Day Foundation, 211 N. 12th St., Lincoln, NE 68410, (402) 474-5655. Tree planting.

❏ Nature Conservancy, 1815 N. Lynn St., Arlington, VA 22209, (703) 841-5300 or (800) 628-6860. Land, water, and wildlife conservation.

❏ Pennsylvania Bureau of Waste Management, Pennsylvania Department of Environmental Resources, P.O. Box 8472, Harrisburg, PA 17105-8472, (717) 787-7382. Recycling hotline is (800) 346-4242.

❏ Plastics Again, 24 Jytek Park, Leominster, MA 01453, (508) 840-1521. Information on starting a plastics-recycling program in your school or community.

❏ Tree People, 12601 Mulholland Dr., Beverly Hills, CA 90210, (818) 753-4600. Tree planting.
❏ Wilderness Society, 900 17th St., NW, Washington, DC 20006, (202) 833-2300.
❏ Wisconsin Department of Natural Resources, P.O. Box 7921, Madison, WI 53707, (608) 267-7565. Recycling; study guides; activity ideas.

Check the White Pages to look up your state and county departments of natural resources, land and waste management bureaus, and other environment-related agencies to see what your region has to offer.

Wildlife and Animal Care

❏ American Association of Zoological Parks and Aquariums, 7970-D Old Georgetown Rd., Bethesda, MD 20814, (301) 907-7777.
❏ American Cetacean Society, P.O. Box 2639, San Pedro, CA 90731, (310) 548-6279. Protection for whales and dolphins.
❏ American Society for the Prevention of Cruelty to Animals (ASPCA), 424 E. 92nd St., New York, NY 10128, (212) 876-7700. Animal shelters; care and adoption programs.
❏ Center for Marine Conservation, 1725 DeSales St., NW, Suite 500, Washington, DC 20036, (202) 429-5609. Beach cleanups and saving sea animals.
❏ The Cousteau Society, 870 Greenbriar Cr., Suite 402, Chesapeake, VA 23320, (804) 523-9335. Marine animals and environment.
❏ Defenders of Wildlife, 1101 14th St. NW, #1400, Washington, DC 20005, (202) 682-9400.
❏ Dian Fossey Gorilla Fund, 45 Inverness Drive East, Suite B, Englewood, CO 80112, (800) 851-0203.
❏ International Wildlife Coalition, 70 E. Falmouth Hwy., East Falmouth, MA 02536-5954, (508) 548-8328. Animal protection and whale adoption programs.
❏ National Audubon Society, 666 Pennsylvania Ave. SE, Washington, DC 20003, (202) 547-9009. All about birds.
❏ National Institute for Urban Wildlife, 10921 Trotting Ridge Way, Columbia, MD 21044, (410) 643-2172. Wildlife conservation in urban and suburban areas.

❑ National Wildlife Federation, 1400 16th St. NW, Washington, DC 20036, (202) 797-6800.
❑ Nature Conservancy. See "Recycling and the Environment."
❑ Pacific Whale Foundation, 101 North Kihei Road, Kihei, HI 96753, (808) 879-8860 or (800) 942-5311. Information and programs for protecting whales.
❑ Recycle for the Birds. See National Wildlife Federation.
❑ Student Action Corps for Animals, P.O. Box 15588, Washington, DC 20003, (202) 543-8983. Animal rights work for students.

Recreation, Arts, and Crafts

Many societies for enthusiasts and collectors are run by amateurs and subject to frequent changes in location. Your best bet for locating, say, the American Malacological Union is to consult a recent directory of hobby and collector organizations, as listed in the publications below.

❑ American Camping Association. See "Disabilities and Illnesses."
❑ American Numismatic Association, 818 N. Cascade Ave., Colorado Springs, CO 80903, (719) 632-2646. Information about coin collecting.
❑ American Philatelic Society, P.O. Box 8000, State College, PA 16803, (814) 237-3803. Information about stamp collecting.
❑ National Endowment for the Arts, Arts and Education Office, 1100 Pennsylvania Ave. NW, Rm. 602, Washington, DC 20506, (202) 682-5400.
❑ Scott Publications, 30595 Eight Mile Rd., Livonia, MI 48152, (810) 477-6650. Information about ceramics and pottery.
❑ S&S Arts and Crafts, 75 Mill St., Colchester, CT 06415, (203) 537-3451 or (800) 937-3482. Publishes a catalog of craft ideas and materials.

Publications

These listings are a good place to start, and they contain some key materials, but they are by no means the last word in what's out there. There are countless useful materials on all of these topics, so be sure to check your local libraries for additional books, articles, and other publications. You may also want to check your phone book for related organizations that can help you locate informational materials.

General Service and the Poor and Homeless

Adams, Patricia, Marzollo, Jean, and Moores, Jeff, *The Helping Hands Handbook: A Guidebook for Kids Who Want to Help People, Animals, and the World We Live in* (New York: Random House, 1992).

Carroll, Andrew, *Volunteer USA* (New York: Fawcett Columbine, 1991).

Catholic Network of Volunteer Service, *The Response* (Washington DC: Catholic Network, 1996).

Commission on Voluntary Service and Action, *Invest Yourself: A Catalogue of Volunteer Opportunities: A Guide to Action* (New York: Commission, 1985).

De Hartog, Jan, *The Hospital* (New York: Atheneum, 1964).

Driver, David, *The Good Heart Book: A Guide to Volunteering* (Chicago: Noble Press, 1989).

Gale Research Company, *The Encyclopedia of Associations* (Detroit: Gale Research Company, 1988).

Gilbert, Sara D., *Lend a Hand: The How, Where, and Why of Volunteering* (New York: Morrow Junior Books, 1988).

Hoose, Phillip M., *It's Our World, Too! Stories of Young People Who Are Making a Difference* (Boston: Joy Street Books, 1993).

Karnes, Frances A., and Bean, Suzanne M., *Girls and Women Leading the Way: Twenty True Stories About Leadership* (Minneapolis: Free Spirit Publishers, 1993).

Kipps, Harriet Clyde, *Volunteerism: The Directory of Organizations, Training, Programs, and Publications* (New Providence NJ: R.R. Bowker, 1991).

Lewis, Barbara A., *The Kid's Guide to Social Action* (Minneapolis: Free Spirit Publishing, 1991).

McPherson, Kate, *Enriching Learning Through Service* (Mt. Vernon, WA: Project Service Leadership, 1992).

Southeastern Regional Vision for Education (SERVE), *Learning by Serving: 2,000 Ideas for Service Learning Projects* (Greensboro: SERVE, Department of Education, University of North Carolina, 1994).

Saccomandi, Pat, and Bobette Reigel Host for the Citizen Volunteer Skillsbank Project, *The Volunteer Skillsbank: An Innovative Way to Connect Individual Talents to Community Needs* (Boulder, CO: Volunteer: The National Center for Citizen Involvement, 1981).

Walls, David, *The Activist's Almanac: The Concerned Citizen's Guide to the Leading Advocacy Organizations in America* (New York: Simon & Schuster, 1993).

Recycling, Environment, Wildlife, and Animal Care

Allison, Linda, *The Sierra Club Summer Book* (New York: Scribners Sons, 1977).

De Bell, Garrett, *The New Environmental Handbook* (San Francisco: Friends of the Earth, 1980).

Earthworks Group, *50 Simple Things Kids Can Do to Save the Earth*, Andrews and McMeel (Kansas City MO, 1990).

Earthworks Group, *The Recycler's Handbook* (Kansas City MO: Earthworks Group, 1990).

Few, Roger, *Macmillan Children's Guide to Endangered Animals* (New York: Maxwell Macmillan International, 1993).

Herman, Marina L., *Teaching Kids to Love the Earth* (Duluth MN: Pfiefer Hamilton Publishers, 1991).

Jabs, Carolyn, *Re-uses: 2133 Ways to Recycle and Reuse the Things You Ordinarily Throw Away* (New York: Crown Publishers, 1982).

Kalbacken, Joan, and Lepthien, Emilie U., *Recycling* (Chicago: Children's Press, 1991).

Lazo, Caroline Evensen, *Endangered Species* (New York: Crestwood House, 1990).

Lefkowitz, R.J., and Johnson, John Emil, *Save It! Keep It! Use It Again! A Book About Conservation and Recycling* (New York: Parents Magazine Press, 1977).

Lowery, Linda, Lorbiecki, Marybeth, and Mataya, David, *Earthwise at Play: A Guide to the Care and Feeding of Your Planet* (Minneapolis: Carolrhoda Books, 1993).

MacEachern, Diane, *Save Our Planet: 750 Everyday Ways You Can Help Clean Up the Earth* (New York: Dell Publishers, 1990).

Miles, Betty, and Nivola, Claire A., *Save the Earth! An Ecology Handbook for Kids* (New York: Knopf, 1974).

Pacific Gas and Electric, *30 Simple Energy Things You Can Do to Save the Earth* (San Francisco: Earthworks Group, 1990).

Penny, Malcolm, and Meadway, Wendy, *Endangered Animals* (New York: Bookwright Press, 1988).

Pringle, Laurence P., *Recycling Resources* (New York: Macmillan Publishers, 1974).

Rafferty, Kevin and Kim, *Kids Gardening: A Kid's Guide to Messing Around in the Dirt* (Palo Alto: Klutz Enterprises, 1989).

Simons, Robin, *Recyclopedia: Games, Science Equipment, and Crafts from Recycled Materials* (Boston: Houghton Mifflin, 1976).

Skidmore, Steve, *What a Load of Trash!* (Brookfield CT: Millbrook Press, 1991).

Smith, Frances C., *The First Book of Conservation* (New York: Watts, 1972).

Viner, Michael, with Hilton, Pat, *365 Ways for You and Your Children to Save the Earth One Day at a Time* (New York: Warner Books, 1991).

Fund-raising

Barkin, Carol, and James, Elizabeth, *Jobs for Kids: The Guide to Having Fun and Making Money* (New York: Lothrop Lee & Shepard Books, 1990).

Drotning, Phillip T., *500 Ways for Small Charities to Raise Money* (Hartsdale NY: Public Service Materials Center, 1981).

Flanagan, Joan, for The Youth Project, *The Grass Roots Fundraising Book: How to Raise Money in Your Community* (Chicago: Contemporary Books, 1982).

Gurin, Maurice G., *What Volunteers Should Know for Successful Fundraising* (New York: Stein and Day, 1980).

Hairston, Martha, and Robertson, James, for Amazing Life Games Co., *Good Cents: Every Kid's Guide to Making Money* (Boston: Houghton Mifflin, 1974).

Reader Mail Department, "101 Surefire Fundraising Ideas," *Family Circle* (October 1976).

Wilkinson, Elizabeth, *Making Cents: Every Kid's Guide to Money* (Boston: Little Brown and Company, 1990).

Publicity

Bortin, Virginia, *Publicity for Volunteers: A Handbook* (New York: Walker, 1981).

Brigham, Nancy, Catalfio, Maria, and Cluster, Dick, *How to Do Leaflets, Newletters and Newspapers* (Detroit New York: PEP Publishers, 1991).

Fletcher, Tana, and Rockler, Julia, *Getting Publicity: A Do-It-Yourself Guide for Small Businesses and Non-Profit Groups* (Vancouver: International Self-Counsel Press, 1990).

Gary Beals Advertising & Public Relations, *Facing The News Media* (San Diego: Gary Beals Advertising, 1990).

Goldstein, Norm, ed., *The Associated Press Stylebook and Libel Manual* (Reading MA: Addison-Wesley, 1992).

Tedone, David, *Practical Publicity: How to Boost Any Cause* (Boston: Harvard Common Press, 1983).

Recreation, Arts, and Crafts

Allard, Denise, and Spomer, Cynthia Russell, *Hobbyist Sourcebook* (Detroit: Gale Research Inc., 1990).

Anderson, Karen C., ed., *Games Magazine Big Book of Games* (New York: Workman Publishing, 1990).

Bergstrom, Joan, *All the Best Contests for Kids* (Berkeley, CA: Ten Speed Press, 1992).

Broekel, Ray, *Aquariums and Terrariums* (Chicago: Children's Press, 1982).

Busch, Akiko, *Wallworks: Creating Unique Environments with Surface Design and Decoration* (New York: Bantam Books, 1988).

Collins, Len, *Card Games for Children* (New York: Barron's, 1989).

Daniels, Harvey, and Turner, Sylvia, *Simple Printmaking with Children* (New York: Van Nostrand Reinhold, 1972).

Hamilton, Katie and Gene, *Build It Together: 27 Easy to Make Woodworking Projects for Adults and Children* (New York: Scribner Book Companies, 1984).

Lerner Publications Co., *Make Your Own Musical Instruments* (Minneapolis: Lerner, 1988).

Orinda Art Council, *Touch with Your Eyes* (Orinda CA: Orinda Art Council, 1990).

Pitcher, Caroline, *Games* (New York: Franklin Watts, 1984).

Utz, Peter, *Do It Yourself Video: A Beginner's Guide to Home Video* (Englewood Cliffs NJ: Prentice-Hall, 1984).

Index

Entries are filed letter by letter. **Boldface** page references indicate main topics. *Italic* page references indicate illustrations and captions.